interchange

FIFTH EDITION

3

Workbook

Jack C. Richards

with Jonathan Hull and Susan Proctor

CAMBRIDGE
UNIVERSITY PRESS

Shaftesbury Road, Cambridge CB2 8EA, United Kingdom

One Liberty Plaza, 20th Floor, New York, NY 10006, USA

477 Williamstown Road, Port Melbourne, VIC 3207, Australia

314–321, 3rd Floor, Plot 3, Splendor Forum, Jasola District Centre, New Delhi – 110025, India

103 Penang Road, #05–06/07, Visioncrest Commercial, Singapore 238467

Torre de los Parques, Colonia Tlacoquemécatl del Valle, Mexico City CP 03200, Mexico

Cambridge University Press & Assessment is a department of the University of Cambridge.

We share the University's mission to contribute to society through the pursuit of education, learning and research at the highest international levels of excellence.

www.cambridge.org
Information on this title: www.cambridge.org/9781316622766

First published 1991
Second edition 1998
Third edition 2005
Fourth edition 2013
Fifth edition 2017
Fifth edition update published 2021

40 39 38 37 36 35 34 33 32 31 30 29 28 27 26 25 24

Printed in Poland by Opolgraf

A catalogue record for this publication is available from the British Library

ISBN 978-1-009-04052-5 Student's Book 3 with eBook
ISBN 978-1-009-04053-2 Student's Book 3A with eBook
ISBN 978-1-009-04054-9 Student's Book 3B with eBook
ISBN 978-1-009-04075-4 Student's Book 3 with Digital Pack
ISBN 978-1-009-04077-8 Student's Book 3A with Digital Pack
ISBN 978-1-009-04078-5 Student's Book 3B with Digital Pack
ISBN 978-1-316-62276-6 Workbook 3
ISBN 978-1-316-62277-3 Workbook 3A
ISBN 978-1-316-62279-7 Workbook 3B
ISBN 978-1-108-40711-3 Teacher's Edition 3
ISBN 978-1-316-62230-8 Class Audio 3
ISBN 978-1-009-04079-2 Full Contact 3 with Digital Pack
ISBN 978-1-009-04080-8 Full Contact 3A with Digital Pack
ISBN 978-1-009-04081-5 Full Contact 3B with Digital Pack
ISBN 978-1-108-40307-8 Presentation Plus 3

Additional resources for this publication at cambridgeone.org

Contents

Credits

The authors and publishers acknowledge the following sources of copyright material and are grateful for the permissions granted. While every effort has been made, it has not always been possible to identify the sources of all the material used, or to trace all copyright holders. If any omissions are brought to our notice, we will be happy to include the appropriate acknowledgements on reprinting and in the next update to the digital edition, as applicable.

Key: BL = Below Left, BR = Below Right, C = Centre, CL = Centre Left, CR = Centre Right, TC = Top Centre, TL = Top Left, TR = Top Right.

Illustrations

337 Jon (KJA Artists): 51; Mark Duffin: 31, 80; Pablo Gallego (Beehive Illustration): 10, 20; Thomas Girard (Good Illustration): 4, 28, 53; Dusan Lakicevic (Beehive Illustration): 1, 14, 22, 33, 96; Yishan Li (Advocate Art): 6, 13, 65; Quino Marin (The Organisation): 29; Gavin Reece (New Division): 3, 64; Paul Williams (Sylvie Poggio Artists): 15, 66.

Photos

Back cover (woman with whiteboard): Jenny Acheson/Stockbyte/GettyImages; Back cover (whiteboard): Nemida/GettyImages; Back cover (man using phone): Betsie Van Der Meer/Taxi/GettyImages; Back cover (woman smiling): PeopleImages.com/DigitalVision/GettyImages; Back cover (name tag): Tetra/Images/GettyImages; Back cover (handshake): David Lees/Taxi/GettyImages; p. 2 : Michael H/DigitalVision/GettyImages; p. 5 (TL): Jade/Blend Images/Getty Images Plus/GettyImages; p. 5 (TR): Jamie Grill/GettyImages; p. 5 (BL): Blend Images - Jose Luis Pelaez Inc/Brand X Pictures/GettyImages; p. 5 (BR): Tomasz Trojanowski/Hemera/Getty Images Plus/GettyImages; p. 7: John Rowley/Photodisc/GettyImages; p. 8: KidStock/Blend Images/GettyImages; p. 9: monkeybusinessimages/iStock/Getty Images Plus/GettyImages; p. 12 (TL): ColorBlind/The Image Bank/GettyImages; p. 12 (TR): Sigrid Gombert/MITO images/GettyImages; p. 12 (CL): 4x6/E+/GettyImages; p. 12 (CR): Roy Hsu/Photographer's Choice RF/GettyImages; p. 13 (TR): mediaphotos/iStock/Getty Images Plus/GettyImages; p. 16: Purestock/GettyImages; p. 17 : PeopleImages/DigitalVision/GettyImages; p. 18: Phil Boorman/Cultura/GettyImages; p. 19 (TL): Robert George Young/Photographer's Choice/GettyImages; p. 19 (BR): dangdumrong/iStock/Getty Images Plus/GettyImages; p. 21 (TR): Chris Dyball/Innerlight/The Image Bank/GettyImages; p. 21 (CL): MattStansfield/iStock/Getty Images Plus/GettyImages; p. 23: EXTREME-PHOTOGRAPHER/E+/GettyImages; p. 24 (Johnson): George Doyle/Stockbyte/GettyImages; p. 24 (Marshall): Digital Vision./Photodisc/GettyImages; p. 24 (James): Yellow Dog Productions/The Image Bank/GettyImages; p. 24 (Grant): wdstock/iStock/Getty Images Plus/GettyImages; p. 24 (Simpson): Dave and Les Jacobs/Blend Images/GettyImages; p. 25 (TR): asiseeit/iStock/Getty Images Plus/GettyImages; p. 25 (BR): hadynyah/E+/GettyImages; p. 26: Thomas_EyeDesign/Vetta/GettyImages; p. 30: Education Images/Universal Images Group/GettyImages; p. 32 (George): snapphoto/E+/GettyImages; p. 32 (airport): Philippe TURPIN/Photononstop/Photolibrary/GettyImages; p. 32 (Diane): Vesnaandjic/E+/GettyImages; p. 32 (car): lisegagne/E+/GettyImages; p. 34: Whiteway/E+/GettyImages; p. 35 (wrench): TokenPhoto/E+/GettyImages; p. 35 (TR): John E. Kelly/Photodisc/GettyImages; p. 36: pixelfusion3d/iStock/Getty Images Plus/GettyImages; p. 37 (drain): belovodchenko/iStock/Getty Images Plus/GettyImages; p. 37 (plane): incposterco/E+/GettyImages; p. 37 (smoke): Harrison Shull/Aurora/GettyImages; p. 37 (land): Sierralara/RooM/GettyImages; p. 38 (forest): Ro-Ma Stock Photography/Photolibrary/GettyImages; p. 39: Howard Shooter/Dorling Kindersley/GettyImages; p. 40: VCG/Contributor/Visual China Group/GettyImages; p. 41: Travel Ink/Gallo Images/The Image Bank/GettyImages; p. 42: SolStock/iStock/Getty Images Plus/GettyImages; p. 43: Doug Armand/Oxford Scientific/GettyImages; p. 44: Wilfried Krecichwost/DigitalVision/GettyImages; p. 45: cglade/E+/GettyImages; p. 46 (TL): Lew Robertson/StockFood Creative/GettyImages; p. 46 (TC): Alina555/iStock/Getty Images Plus/GettyImages; p. 46 (TR): Jose Luis Pelaez Inc/Blend Images/GettyImages; p. 47 (photo 1): Hemera Technologies/PhotoObjects.net/Getty Images Plus/GettyImages; p. 47 (photo 2): Picturenet/Blend Images/GettyImages; p. 47 (photo 3): Zoran Milich/Photodisc/GettyImages; p.47 (photo 4): DragonImages/iStock/Getty Images Plus/GettyImages; p. 48 (TR): BrianAJackson/iStock/Getty Images Plus/GettyImages; p. 48 (CR): reka prod./Westend61/GettyImages; p. 49 (TR): simazoran/iStock/Getty Images Plus/Getty Image; p. 49 (CR): ONOKY - Eric Audras/Brand X Pictures/GettyImages; p. 49 (BR): michaeljung/iStock/Getty Images Plus/GettyImages; p. 50: leaf/iStock/Getty Images Plus/GettyImages; p. 52 (TL): IP Galanternik D.U./E+/GettyImages; p. 52 (TR): Lady-Photo/iStock/Getty Images Plus/GettyImages; p. 54: Westend61/GettyImages; p. 55 (CR): Andy Sheppard/Redferns/GettyImages; p. 55 (BR): by Roberto Peradotto/Moment/GettyImages; p. 56 (L): Mint/Hindustan Times/GettyImages; p. 56 (R): Michael Runkel/imageBROKER/GettyImages; p. 57: Bettmann/GettyImages; p. 58 (TL): Bettmann/GettyImages; p. 58 (BR): Ron Levine/Photographer's Choice/GettyImages; p. 59: Windsor & Wiehahn/Stone/GettyImages; p. 60: Javier Pierini/Stone/GettyImages; p. 61: blackred/iStock/Getty Images Plus/GettyImages; p. 62: izusek/iStock/Getty Images Plus/GettyImages; p. 63: ADRIAN DENNIS/AFP/GettyImages; p. 67: Greg Vaughn/Perspectives/GettyImages; p. 68: Caiaimage/Robert Daly/GettyImages; p. 69 (TL): marco wong/Moment/GettyImages; p. 69 (TR): Oscar Wong/Moment Open/GettyImages; p. 69 (CL): Otto Stadler/Photographer's Choice/GettyImages; p. 69 (CR): David Hannah/Lonely Planet Images/GettyImages; p. 69 (BL): LOOK Photography/UpperCut Images/GettyImages; p. 69 (BR): lightkey/E+/GettyImages; p. 70: Thomas Kokta/Photographer's Choice RF/GettyImages; p. 71 (Calgary Farmers' Market): Ken Woo/Calgary Farmers' Market; p. 71 (WWF): © naturepl.com/Andy Rouse/WWF; p. 72: Christian Hoehn/Taxi/GettyImages; p. 73 (TL): Rosanna U/Image Source/GettyImages; p. 73 (TC): Mark Weiss/Photodisc/GettyImages; p. 73 (TR): i love images/Cultura/GettyImages; p. 73 (BL): monkeybusinessimages/iStock/Getty Images Plus/GettyImages; p. 73 (BC): Photo and Co/The Image Bank/GettyImages; p. 73 (BR): Alija/E+/GettyImages; p. 74 (stonehenge): Maxine Bolton/EyeEm/GettyImages; p. 74 (people): Peter Dennis/GettyImages; p. 74 (boats): De Agostini/M. Seemuller/De Agostini Picture Library/GettyImages; p. 75 (bigfoot): Big_Ryan/DigitalVision Vectors/GettyImages; p. 75 (footprints): Danita Delimont/Gallo Images/GettyImages; p. 76: Steve Bronstein/Stone/GettyImages; p. 77: kbeis/DigitalVision Vectors/GettyImages; p. 78: mediaphotos/Vetta/GettyImages; p. 79 (T): Oscar Garces/CON/LatinContent Editorial/GettyImages; p. 81: Theo Wargo/Getty Images North America/GettyImages; p. 82 (TL): ColorBlind Images/Blend Images/GettyImages; p. 82 (TR): track5/E+/GettyImages; p. 83: imagenavi/GettyImages; p. 84 (TL): John Wildgoose/Caiaimage/GettyImages; p. 84 (TR): Bloomberg/GettyImages; p. 84 (CL): Chris Ryan/Caiaimage/GettyImages; p. 84 (CR): numbeos/E+/GettyImages; p. 84 (BL): Tom Merton/OJO Images/GettyImages; p. 84 (BR): Ariel Skelley/Blend Images/GettyImages; p. 85 (TL): marcoventuriniautieri/E+/GettyImages; p. 85 (TR): Anadolu Agency/GettyImages; p. 85 (CL): Caspar Benson/GettyImages; p. 85 (CR): Jake Olson Studios Blair Nebraska/Moment/GettyImages; p. 86 (house): Peter Baker/GettyImages; p. 86 (traffic): Levi Bianco/Moment/GettyImages; p. 86 (bike): Billy Hustace/The Image Bank/GettyImages; p. 86 (using mobile): SolStock/E+/GettyImages; p. 87: Image Source/DigitalVision/GettyImages; p. 89: Caiaimage/Paul Bradbury/Riser/GettyImages; p. 90: Dawid Garwol/EyeEm/GettyImages; p. 92: FatCamera/E+/GettyImages; p. 93: c.Zeitgeist/Everett/REX/Shutterstock; p. 94 (TR): shapecharge/E+/GettyImages; p. 94 (BR): borgogniels/iStock/Getty Images Plus/GettyImages; p. 95: Lucidio Studio, Inc./Moment/GettyImages.

1 That's my kind of friend!

1 Complete these descriptions with the words from the list.

1. Eric is so ___modest___! He always has such great ideas and never takes any credit for them.

2. The Wongs like meeting new people and having friends over for dinner. They're one of the most _____ couples I know.

3. You can't trust Alice. She always promises to do something, but then she never does it. She's pretty _____.

4. James wants to be an actor. It's hard to break into the business, but his family is very _____ of his dream.

5. I never know how to act around Lisa! One minute she's in a good mood, and the next minute she's in a bad mood. She's so _____.

✓	modest
☐	outgoing
☐	supportive
☐	temperamental
☐	unreliable

2 Opposites

A Complete the chart by forming the opposites of the adjectives in the list. Use *in-* and *un-*. Then check your answers in a dictionary.

✓ attractive	☐ dependent	☐ formal
☐ reasonable	✓ competent	☐ experienced
☐ helpful	☐ reliable	☐ cooperative
☐ flexible	☐ popular	☐ sensitive

Opposites with *in-*		Opposites with *un-*	
incompetent	_____	unattractive	_____
_____	_____	_____	_____
_____	_____	_____	_____

incompetent

B Write four more sentences using any of the words in part A.

1. Alan is very incompetent at work. He makes a lot of mistakes.

2. _____

3. _____

4. _____

5. _____

3 Add *who* or *that* to the conversation where necessary.
Put an *X* where *who* or *that* is not necessary.

A: I'm looking for someone _____*X*_____ I can go on vacation with.

B: Hmm. So what kind of person are you looking for?

A: I want to travel with someone _____ is easygoing and independent.

B: Right. And you'd probably also like a person _____ is reliable.

A: Yeah, and I want someone _____ I know well.

B: So why don't you ask me?

A: You? I know you too well!

B: Ha! Does that mean you think I'm someone _____ is high-strung, dependent, and unreliable?

A: No! I'm just kidding. You're definitely someone _____ I could go on vacation with. So, . . . what are you doing in June?

4 Complete the sentences with *who* or *that* and your own information or ideas.

1. I generally like to go out with people <u>who are easygoing and have a sense of humor</u> .

2. I'd rather travel with someone _____ .

3. I don't really want a roommate _____ .

4. My classmates and I like teachers _____ .

5. My best friend and I want to meet people _____ .

6. Most workers would prefer a boss _____ .

7. Some people don't like stingy types _____ .

8. I don't want to have inflexible friends _____ .

9. I feel comfortable discussing my problems with friends _____ .

10. My favorite friends are people _____ .

5 Two of a kind?

A Read the article. What six personality types are discussed?

DO OPPOSITES ATTRACT EACH OTHER?

Some psychologists believe that we are attracted to people who seem to have the characteristics that we wish we had. For example, if you love music but don't play an instrument, you might be attracted to someone who is a musician. Being with that person allows you to be close to something that is important to you and that you want more of in your life.

Because people are very complex, we can be attracted to several different kinds of people who are our opposites in one way or another. So let's take a look at six principal kinds of characteristics in people, and you can decide which type you are most like and which type is your opposite.

Let's begin with introverted and extroverted people. Introverted people often spend a lot of time inside their minds and can be quiet and reserved. Extroverted people enjoy getting out and spending time with other people. If opposites attract, then there will always be an interest between introverted and extroverted people. Introverted people will get out of their minds and into the world with their extroverted friends or partners, while extroverted people will appreciate the quiet space of the inner world of their introverted friends or partners.

Then there are people who relate to the world from a thinking perspective and others who relate to it from a feeling perspective. Thinkers can be cool and objective in their judgments, while feelers may be warm and passionate about theirs. Because people who spend a lot of time thinking want to feel deeply too, they may be attracted to a feeling kind of person. And someone who is very aware of their own powerful feelings may enjoy the company of a relaxed and logical thinker.

Two other characteristics are those of people who use their five senses to understand the world we live in as opposed to those who use their intuition. Sensing people are very aware of the present moment; they are realistic and practical people. Intuitive people, on the other hand, often spend their time in a future of infinite possibilities where their imagination is as free as a bird. The attraction here could be that intuitive people realize they need the practical know-how of sensing people in order to make their dreams come true. Likewise, the sensors are attracted to the imaginative possibilities they see in intuitive people.

These three different pairs of personality characteristics – the introvert and the extrovert, the thinker and the feeler, and the sensor and the intuitive – are of course found in each individual person. Yet many psychologists believe that a person will more often use one characteristic of each pair, in the same way that people use either their left hand or their right. And, according to the idea that opposites attract, the left hand needs the right hand in the same way that the right hand needs the left!

B Based on the information in the article, what kind of people are you attracted to? Circle the words. Then, using the idea that opposites attract, complete the next sentence with the type of person *you* must be.

1. I am more attracted to a person who is (introverted / extroverted). Therefore, I am _____.

2. I am more attracted to a person who is a (thinker / feeler). Therefore, I am a _____.

3. I am more attracted to a person who is the (sensing type / intuitive type). Therefore, I am a _____.

C Do you agree with the kind of person you seem to be according to part B? Why or why not?

_____

6 Match the clauses in column A with the most suitable clauses in column B.

A	B
1. I like it _____	**a.** when someone criticizes me in front of other people.
2. I don't mind it _____	**b.** when people are easygoing and friendly.
3. It upsets me _____	**c.** when rich people are stingy.
4. It embarrasses me _____	**d.** when people are a few minutes late for an appointment.

7 Write sentences about these situations. Use the expressions in the box.

I love it . . .   I can't stand it . . .   I don't like it . . .
It upsets me . . .   It bothers me . . .   I don't mind it . . .
I really like it . . .   It makes me happy . . .   It makes me angry . . .

1. _I don't like it when people cut in line._

2. _____

3. _____

4. _____

5. _____

6. _____

8 What are some things you like and don't like about people? Write two sentences about each of the following. Use the ideas in the pictures and your own ideas.

1. What I really like:

I love it when someone

is generous and gives me flowers.

It makes me happy when

_____

2. What I don't like:

It bothers me when

_____

_____

_____

3. What doesn't bother me:

I don't mind it when

_____

_____

_____

4. What upsets me:

It upsets me when

_____

_____

_____

9 It really bugs me!

Choose one thing from Exercise 8 that really embarrasses, bothers, or upsets you. Write two paragraphs about it. In the first paragraph, describe the situation. In the second paragraph, say why this situation is difficult for you and describe a situation you would prefer.

It really embarrasses me when someone is too generous to me. Recently, I dated a guy who was always giving me things. For my birthday, he bought me an expensive necklace, and he treated me to dinner and a movie.

The problem is, I don't have enough money to treat him in the same way. I'd prefer to date someone I have more in common with. In fact, my ideal boyfriend is someone who is sensible and saves his money!

_____
_____
_____
_____
_____
_____
_____
_____
_____

10 Choose the correct word to complete each sentence.

1. I can tell Simon anything, and I know he won't tell anyone else. I can really _____ him.
   (believe / treat / trust)

2. Kay has a very high opinion of herself. I don't like people who are so _____.
   (egotistical / temperamental / supportive)

3. It bothers me when people are too serious. I prefer people who are _____ and have a good sense of humor. (easygoing / inflexible / reliable)

4. I like it when someone expresses strong _____. Hearing other people's views can really make you think. (accomplishments / compliments / opinions)

5. Lisa is very rich, but she only spends her money on herself. She's very _____.
   (generous / modest / stingy)

2 Working 9 to 5

1 What's your job?

A Match the jobs with their definitions.

A/An . . .	is a person who . . . .
1. comedian __f__	**a.** researches environmentally friendly technologies
2. green researcher _____	**b.** helps students with their problems
3. guidance counselor _____	**c.** controls a company's brand online
4. organic food farmer _____	**d.** creates computer applications
5. social media manager _____	**e.** grows food without chemicals
6. software developer _____	**f.** makes people laugh for a living

B Write a definition for each of these jobs: accountant, fashion designer, and flight attendant.

1. _An accountant is someone who_ _____

2. _____

3. _____

2 Challenging or frightening?

A Which words have a positive meaning, and which ones have a negative meaning? Write *P* or *N*.

awful __N__   fantastic _____

boring _____   fascinating _____

challenging _____   frightening _____

dangerous _____   interesting _____

difficult _____   rewarding _____

B Write about four more jobs you know. Use the words in part A and gerund phrases.

1. _I think being a comedian would be fascinating._ _____

2. _____

3. _____

4. _____

5. _____

3 Career choices

A Match each career and the most appropriate job responsibility.

Careers		Job responsibilities
work	for an airline	do research
	with computers	teach discipline and fitness
	as a high school coach	learn new software programs
be	a university professor	work independently
	a writer	travel to different countries

B Use the information from part A and gerund phrases to complete this conversation.

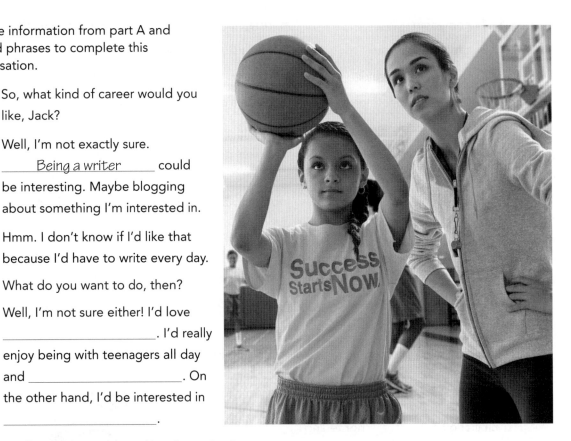

Teri: So, what kind of career would you like, Jack?

Jack: Well, I'm not exactly sure. _____Being a writer_____ could be interesting. Maybe blogging about something I'm interested in.

Teri: Hmm. I don't know if I'd like that because I'd have to write every day.

Jack: What do you want to do, then?

Teri: Well, I'm not sure either! I'd love _____. I'd really enjoy being with teenagers all day and _____. On the other hand, I'd be interested in _____.

Jack: Really? What would you like about that?

Teri: Well, I'd love _____ all over the world.

Jack: Oh, I could never do that! I think it would be very tiring work.

C Write a short conversation like the one in part B. Use the remaining information in part A or your own ideas.

A: So, what kind of career would you like?

B: Well, I'm not exactly sure. _____

A: That sounds interesting. But I wouldn't like it because _____

B: What do you want to do then?

A: Well, I'd love _____

B: _____

A: _____

4 What a job!

A Read the magazine interviews. Write the correct job title above each interview. There are two extra jobs.

- ☐ architect
- ☐ bus driver
- ☐ freelance artist
- ☐ house painter
- ☐ preschool teacher
- ☐ train conductor
- ☐ university professor
- ☐ website designer

TELL US ABOUT YOUR JOB

1 _____

I have always enjoyed making things, and what's more interesting than building something that people will use for years? The challenge of discovering exactly how a space needs to be constructed for maximum usefulness and beauty is what makes me wake up with a smile. I often work late at the office, but that's part of the job.

2 _____

Working for yourself is hard because you're responsible for everything. If no one calls you and asks you to work for them, you have to go out and look for work. Luckily, I now have some regular clients. I paint pictures for some expensive hotels. Right now, I'm doing some paintings for the rooms of a new hotel in Hawaii.

3 _____

My friends say my work is less demanding than theirs, but I work just as hard as they do. I spend a lot of time alone because my job can't begin until all the construction work is completed. Usually, the rooms look great when I've finished my work. Sometimes I don't like the colors that customers choose, but I have to do what they want.

4 _____

These days a lot of people are doing what I've been doing for fifteen years. I work closely with my clients to find out exactly what they want to show on the Internet and how to make it look as attractive as possible. My work requires a good eye for art, a command of clear and precise language, and of course, knowledge of the latest technology.

5 _____

I meet all kinds of people: some are the best and others aren't so good. Sometimes I have a great conversation with someone I've never met before. And of course, I have my regulars, people I see every day, and we talk about life. But I always keep my attention on the road.

6 _____

Being with kids all day isn't for everyone, but I love it. I take care of children when their parents are away. I do all kinds of things – I teach, I play games, and I read books. I make sure the children are safe and happy. I have a lot of responsibility, but I love my job. It's very rewarding work even though the pay isn't great.

B Underline the words and phrases that helped you find the answers in part A.

5

First, use words from the list to complete each job title.
Then choose the best expressions to compare the jobs in each sentence.

☐ assistant   ☐ decorator   ☐ painter   ☐ walker
☐ counselor   ☐ instructor   ☐ ranger   ✓ worker

1. A child-care _____ worker _____ doesn't earn _____ as much as _____ an accountant.
   - ✓ as much as   ☐ greater than   ☐ worse than

2. A chef's _____ has _____ a waiter.
   - ☐ worse hours than   ☐ not as good hours   ☐ as worse hours as

3. A dog _____ is _____ a student intern.
   - ☐ more interesting than   ☐ not as boring as   ☐ better paid than

4. A house _____ earns _____ a camp counselor.
   - ☐ as bad as   ☐ more than   ☐ not more than

5. A park _____ is _____ a landscaper.
   - ☐ as bad as   ☐ not as well paid as   ☐ worse than

6. Being a yoga _____ is _____ being a professor.
   - ☐ more than   ☐ as much as   ☐ not as difficult as

7. Being an interior _____ is _____ being a sales assistant.
   - ☐ greater than   ☐ earns more than   ☐ more interesting than

8. A guidance _____ has _____ a gardener.
   - ☐ more responsibility than   ☐ not more than   ☐ not as long as

6

Complete these sentences with the correct prepositions.
Some of the prepositions may be used more than once.
More than one answer may be possible.

☐ as
☐ at
☐ in
☐ on
☐ with

1. Chonglin works _____ the best Chinese restaurant in Los Angeles.

2. I think working _____ other people is more fun than working alone.

3. I would hate working _____ the media. It would be nerve-racking!

4. Working _____ a dance instructor sounds great.

5. Working _____ an office is less interesting than working _____ a cruise ship.

7 Use the words in parentheses to compare the jobs.

Assistant needed at an outdoor swimming pool. Must be able to swim. Responsible for keeping pool and changing rooms clean. $12/hour. Tues.–Fri. 12–7.

Learn web design!
In search of a bright young person to work as an intern for an advertising agency. Some clerical work. $15/hour. Mon.–Fri. 9–5.

1. **A:** _An assistant at a swimming pool has shorter hours than an intern._
   (shorter hours)

   B: _Yes, but working as an intern is more interesting than being a swimming pool assistant._
   (interesting)

Travel agency needs energetic people. Knowledge of a second language is a plus. Mostly answering the phone. $18/hour. Flexible hours. Five vacation days a year.

Tutors in math, science, English, and music wanted at private summer school. Challenging work with gifted teenagers. Salary negotiable. Mon.–Sat. 3–7.

2. **A:** _Working in a_ _____
   (better benefits)

   B: _Yes, but working_ _____
   (challenging)

Tennis instructor needed at summer camp for 12- and 13-year-olds. Must be excellent tennis player and good with kids. $18/hour. Mon.–Fri. 1–7.

Tour company seeks **guide** to lead bus tours. Great attitude and good speaking voice a must! Fun work, but must be willing to work long hours. $15/hour.

3. **A:** _____
   (make as much money)

   B: _____
   (work longer hours)

City seeks **taxi drivers** for morning shift. No experience necessary; driver's license required. $15/hour plus tips. Mon.–Thu. 7 A.M.–2 P.M.

Office assistant required in small, friendly office. Computer skills an advantage. Interesting work. Some management skills necessary. $20/hour. 6-day week.

4. **A:** _____
   (a shorter work week)

   B: _____
   (less boring)

8 Choose four pairs of jobs from the box below to compare.
Say which job you would prefer and give two reasons.

- a graphic designer/a TV news director
- an architect/a teacher
- a guidance counselor/a coach
- a doctor/a musician

- a police officer/a politician
- a secret agent/a psychiatrist
- working on a construction site/working in an office
- being self-employed/working for a company

Example: Working as a TV news director sounds more interesting than being a graphic designer.
A TV news director has more responsibility than a graphic designer.
Also, directing the news is better paid.

1. _____

_____

_____

2. _____

_____

_____

3. _____

_____

_____

4. _____

_____

_____

3 Lend a hand.

1 Would you mind . . . ?

A Complete the request for each situation.

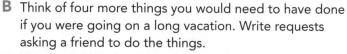

1. You want to borrow a classmate's pen.

  <u>Can I borrow your pen?</u>

2. You want a classmate to give you a ride home after class.

  <u>Would you mind</u>

3. You want to turn down your roommate's TV.

  <u>Is it OK if</u>

4. You want to use a friend's cell phone.

  <u>Do you mind if</u>

5. You want to borrow a friend's car for the weekend.

  <u>I was wondering if</u>

6. You want someone to tell you how to get to the subway.

  <u>Could</u>

B Think of four more things you would need to have done if you were going on a long vacation. Write requests asking a friend to do the things.

1. <u>Could you water the plants?</u>

2. _____

3. _____

4. _____

5. _____

2 Accept or decline these requests. For requests you decline, give excuses. Use the expressions in the chart or expressions of your own.

Accepting	Declining
That's OK, I guess.	Sorry, but . . .
I'd be glad to.	I'd like to, but . . .
Fine. No problem.	Unfortunately, . . .

1. **A:** Can I use your computer? My computer crashed.

   B: _Sorry, but I'm going to use it myself in a few minutes._

2. **A:** I've just finished this ten-page paper. Could you check it for me, please?

   B: _____

3. **A:** I was wondering if I could stay at your place for a week while my landlord fixes the roof.

   B: _____

4. **A:** Would you mind if I used your cell phone to make a long-distance call to Nigeria?

   B: _____

3 Look at the pictures and write the conversations. Speaker A makes a request. Speaker B declines it. Each speaker should give a reason.

1. **A:** _Could you carry these boxes_
   for me? I have a bad back.

   B: _Sorry, but I have a bad back, too._
   _____

2. **A:** _____
   _____

   B: _____
   _____

3. **A:** _____
   _____

   B: _____
   _____

4 Getting what you want

A Scan the magazine article about making requests. What strategies can you use for less formal requests? What strategies can you use for more formal requests?

The Art of Making Requests

When you make a request, it helps to be clear about two things: Firstly, how well do you know the other person? Secondly, how important is it for you to get what you want? Are you willing to take "no" for an answer?

Let's say that you would like to borrow someone's car to go out on Friday night. Because borrowing a car is a big favor, we can assume that you'd probably only ask someone you know well for this favor. In general, when making requests of friends or close acquaintances, you can use a less formal approach.

Now let's imagine that it's very important for you to have that car on Friday night; you have to have it. In that case, you can let the other person know in a less formal, direct way. Here are two possible strategies:

1. Make a statement with *need*: "I need to borrow your car."
2. Use an imperative: "Please lend me your car."

By avoiding questions, this approach makes it more difficult for the other person to say no. If you are willing to put the other person in a possibly awkward situation, then this is definitely the clearest, and perhaps most effective, way of getting what you want.

But maybe you expect the other person to say no, and you can live with that. This attitude allows you to have a cooler, more objective perspective, so you can make your request in a more formal, indirect way.

Here are some examples:

3. Ask about ability: "Could/Can you lend me your car?"
4. Be polite – use *may*: "May I borrow your car?"
5. Ask for permission: "Would it be OK if I borrowed your car?"
6. Express curiosity: "I wonder if I could borrow your car."
7. State the request negatively: "I don't suppose you could lend me your car."
8. Apologize: "I hope you don't mind my asking, but could I borrow your car?"
9. Give a hint: "I have plans for Friday night, but I don't have a car."

This approach gives the other person a polite way to refuse if, for any reason, they don't want to or cannot lend you their car. And even though you know the person well, taking a more formal approach proves to the listener that you realize what a big favor you're asking. It shows them respect and appreciation – which makes it more likely that you'll get the result you want!

B Read the article. Check (✓) if each request is less formal or more formal. Then write the correct number from the article (1–9) for each type of request. Only eight of the numbers will be used.

	Less formal	More formal	Type
1. Close the door.	☐	☐	____
2. It's really cold in here.	☐	☐	____
3. Could you possibly move your car?	☐	☐	____
4. May I borrow your dictionary?	☐	☐	____
5. I was wondering if you could help me with this assignment.	☐	☐	____
6. I need some help moving to my new apartment.	☐	☐	____
7. I'm sorry, but I can't stand loud music.	☐	☐	____
8. I don't suppose I could borrow your camera.	☐	☐	____

5 Nouns and verbs

A Complete this chart. Then check your answers in a dictionary.

Noun	Verb	Noun	Verb
apology	_apologize_	invitation	_____
compliment	_____	permission	_____
explanation	_____	request	_____

B Check (✓) the phrase that describes what each person is doing.

1. Don't worry. I know you didn't mean to break it.
   - ☐ returning a favor
   - ☐ accepting an apology

2. I really like your new haircut.
   - ☐ giving a reason
   - ☐ giving a compliment

3. Can I borrow your laptop?
   - ☐ asking for a favor
   - ☐ giving a gift

4. I can't lend you my bike because I need it myself.
   - ☐ declining a request
   - ☐ accepting an invitation

5. Could you help me cook dinner?
   - ☐ making a request
   - ☐ returning a compliment

6 Choose the correct words.

1. My phone didn't work for a week. The phone company _____ an apology and took $20 off my bill. (accepted / denied / offered)

2. A friend of mine really loves to _____ compliments, but he never gives anyone else one. I don't understand why he's like that. (do / owe / receive)

3. Diane is always talking on the phone. She makes a lot of calls, but she rarely _____ mine. Maybe she never listens to her voice mail! (makes / offers / returns)

4. I need to _____ a favor. Could you please give me a ride to school tomorrow? My bike has a flat tire! (ask for / give / turn down)

7 **Use these messages to complete the phone conversations. Use indirect requests.**

———— Message ————

For: Silvia

Ms. Karen Landers called. Her flight arrives at 7 P.M. on Tuesday. Please meet her in the International Arrivals area.

———— Message ————

For: Mike

Mr. Maxwell called yesterday. The meeting is on Thursday at 10:30 A.M. Don't forget to bring your report.

———— Message ————

For: Mark

Ed called this morning. Can he borrow your scanner? If he can, when can he pick it up?

———— Message ————

For: Katy

Andy Chow called earlier. Are you going to the conference tomorrow? What time does it start?

1. A: Is Silvia Vega there, please?

   B: No, she isn't. Would you like to leave a message?

   A: Yes, please. This is Karen Landers calling from Toronto.

      Could you tell her _that my flight arrives at 7 P.M. on Tuesday_____ ?

      Would _____ ?

   B: OK, I'll give her the message.

2. A: Can I speak to Mark, please?

   B: I'm afraid he's not here. Do you want to leave a message?

   A: Yes, please. This is Ed. Please _____ .

      And if it's OK, could you _____ ?

   B: Sure, I'll leave him the message.

3. A: Could I speak to Mike, please?

   B: I'm sorry, but he's not here right now.

   A: Oh, OK. This is Mr. Maxwell. I'd like to leave a message.

      Could _____ ?

      Could _____ ?

4. A: I'd like to speak to Katy, please.

   B: She's not here right now. Can I take a message?

   A: Yeah. This is Andy Chow.

      Can _____ ?

      And would _____ ?

   B: OK, I'll give Katy your message.

8 Complete the conversation with the information in the box. Add any words necessary and use the correct form of the verbs given.

☐ ask Kelly to get some soda   ☐ bring a big salad
☐ borrow some money   ☐ buy dessert
☑ borrow your wireless speaker   ☐ don't be late

Dan: So, is there anything I can do to help for the party?

Mark: Yeah. I have a list here. Would it be all right
if I borrowed your wireless speaker?
Mine isn't working very well.

Dan: Sure. And I'll bring two extra speakers. We'll have
amazing sound.

Mark: Thanks.

Dan: No problem. Now, what about food?

Mark: Well, I thought maybe a salad. Would you mind _____,
too?

Dan: Well, OK. And how about drinks?

Mark: Well, could you _____? And please tell her
_____. Last time we had a party, she didn't arrive till
eleven o'clock, and everyone got really thirsty!

Dan: I remember.

Mark: One more thing – I was wondering if you could _____.

Dan: Um, sure. All right. But, uh, would you mind if I _____ to
pay for it?

9 Rewrite these sentences. Find another way to say each sentence using the words given.

1. Can I use your cell phone?
   Would it be OK if I used your cell phone? (OK)

2. Please ask Annie to stop by and talk to me.
   _____ (would)

3. Could I borrow your guitar?
   _____ (wonder)

4. Would you ask Mitch what time he's coming over?
   _____ (could / when)

5. Lend me your hairbrush.
   _____ (mind)

4 What happened?

1 Complete these news stories using the verbs from the box.

1.

| ☐ broke | ☐ found | ☐ locking | ☐ stayed | ☑ went |
| ☐ drank | ☐ heard | ☐ shouted | ☐ waiting | ☐ wondered |

WOMAN TRAPPED IN BATHROOM FOR 20 DAYS

A 69-year-old grandmother in Paris ____went____ to the bathroom – and _____ there for twenty days. What happened? As she was _____ the door, the lock _____. She could not open the door. She _____ for help, but no one _____ her because her bathroom had no windows. After nearly three weeks, the woman's neighbors _____ where she was. Firefighters broke into her apartment and _____ her in a "very weakened" state. While she was _____ to be rescued, she _____ warm water.

2.

| ☐ became | ☐ checking in | ☐ entered | ☐ opened | ☐ sleeping |
| ☐ behaving | ☐ decided | ☐ had | ☐ showed | |

TIGER CUB FOUND IN LUGGAGE

A woman was _____ strangely when she _____ the Bangkok airport. While she was _____ for an overseas flight, she _____ difficulty with a very large bag. The check-in clerk _____ suspicious and _____ to X-ray the bag. The X-ray _____ an image that looked like an animal. When airport staff _____ the bag, they saw that a baby tiger was _____ under lots of toy tigers. The tiger was taken to a rescue center for wildlife, and the woman was arrested.

2 Join each sentence in column A with an appropriate sentence in column B. Use *as*, *when*, or *while* to join the sentences.

A	B
I was crossing the road.	My racket broke.
I was using my computer.	A car nearly hit me.
We were playing tennis.	The water got cold.
I was taking a shower.	I burned my finger.
I was cooking dinner.	It suddenly stopped working.

1. As I was crossing the road, a car nearly hit me.
2. _____
3. _____
4. _____
5. _____

3 Complete these conversations. Use the simple past or the past continuous of the verbs given.

1. **A:** Guess what happened to me last night! As I __was getting__ (get) into bed, I _____ (hear) a loud noise like a gunshot in the street. Then the phone _____ (ring).

   B: Who was it?

   A: It was Luisa. She always calls me late at night, but this time she had a reason. She _____ (drive) right past my apartment when she _____ (get) a flat tire. It was very late, so while we _____ (change) the tire, I _____ (invite) her to spend the night.

2. **A:** I'm sorry I'm so late, Erin. I was at the dentist.

   B: Don't tell me! While you _____ (sit) in the waiting room, you _____ (meet) someone interesting. I know how you are, Matt!

   A: Well, you're wrong this time. The dentist _____ (clean) my teeth when she suddenly _____ (get) called away for an emergency. So I just sat there waiting for two hours with my mouth hanging open!

A Read this news story. Who is it about? Where did it take place?

Thank you, Andre Botha!

Surfing at the Pipeline

On December 6, 2015, Andre Botha was in the water, watching the big waves at the Pipeline off the island of Oahu, Hawaii, when he noticed something strange. The two-time world bodyboarding champion realized that professional champion surfer Evan Geiselman was in big trouble. Since the Pipeline has some of the biggest waves in the world and is considered to be the most dangerous place on the planet for surfing, situations like this are, unfortunately, not uncommon.

Botha realized that the surfer, who had entered the inside of a huge wave and was riding it, was knocked off his surfboard when the wave crashed on him. Normally a surfer will come up to the surface of the water a few moments after falling off the board. But there was no sign of Geiselman. Botha began to swim on his bodyboard as fast as he could to where the surfboard was being thrown around by the huge waves. When he reached the surfboard, he saw Geiselman, who looked like he might be dead. The surfer was unconscious and his face was turning blue as Botha tried to bring him back to life in the water. Botha breathed into Geiselman's mouth and hit him on the chest to get him breathing again. Then he began to swim to shore with the surfer's unconscious body. Two lifeguards swam out to meet him, and they brought Geiselman to a hospital.

Surfers and bodyboarders agree that Evan Geiselman would probably not be alive today if Andre Botha had not rescued him. They don't always agree about which sport is best, but surfers and bodyboarders do agree that taking care of each other in the big waves is important. This respect and care for people is a wonderful part of these exciting sports.

Bodyboarding

B Use the article to answer these questions.

1. In what sport is Andre Botha a two-time champion?

_____

2. What sport does Evan Geiselman excel at as a champion?

_____

3. Where is the Pipeline located?

_____

4. What is one way you can help an unconscious person start breathing?

_____

5. Who brought Geiselman to the hospital?

_____

6. What helps make bodyboarding and surfing such wonderful sports?

_____

5 Think of a real or imaginary problem like the one in Exercise 4. Write two paragraphs. In the first paragraph, describe your problem. In the second, say how you solved it.

_____
_____
_____
_____
_____
_____
_____
_____
_____
_____
_____
_____

> A couple of years ago, I got lost in the mountains. I was hiking when it suddenly got foggy. I was really frightened because I couldn't see anything, and it was getting cold. I decided to put up my tent and stay there for the night.
>
> While I was putting up my tent, though, the fog began to clear. . . .

6 Choose the correct verbs to complete the story.

Grammar note: After

In sentences using *after* that show one past event occurring before another, the clause with *after* usually uses the past perfect.
After she **had called** her friend, her cell phone battery died.

Andy and I ___had just gotten___ engaged, so we
　　　　(just got / had just gotten)

went to a jewelry store to buy a wedding ring. We _____ a ring when a
　　　　　　　　　　　　　　　　　　　　　　　　　(just chose / had just chosen)

masked man _____. After the robber _____ Andy's
　　　　(came in / had come in)　　　　　　　　　　　　(took / had taken)

wallet, he _____ the ring. I _____ it to him when the
　　(demanded / had demanded)　　(just handed / had just handed)

alarm _____ to go off, and the robber _____. We were
　　(started / had started)　　　　　　　　　　　　(ran off / had run off)

so relieved! But then the sales assistant _____ us we had to pay for the ring
　　　　　　　　　　　　　　　　　　　　(told / had told)

because I _____ it to the robber. We _____ her
　　(gave / had given)　　　　　　　　　　(just told / had just told)

that we wouldn't pay for it when the police _____ and
　　　　　　　　　　　　　　　　　　　　(arrived / had arrived)

_____ us! What a terrible experience!
(arrested / had arrested)

7 What a story!

A Choose the best headline for each of these news stories.

What a disaster! **What a triumph!**

What an emergency! **What a lucky break!** **What a dilemma!**

1. _____

Karen Lane was seven months pregnant when she and her husband, Scott, went on vacation to a small **remote** island off the coast of South America. On the first night, Karen was in a lot of pain. There were no doctors on the island, so Scott called a hospital on the **mainland**. They told him they could not send a helicopter because a typhoon was coming. During the night, Karen thought she was going to die. Luckily, the typhoon had passed over the island by the following morning. A helicopter picked Karen up and took her to the hospital – just in time for her to have a beautiful baby girl.

2. _____

Serena Mills was very sick for several months before her final exams this summer. She couldn't study at all. Her parents suggested she should **skip** a year and take the exams the next summer. **Remarkably**, Serena suddenly got well just before the exams, spent two weeks studying, and got the highest grade in her class!

3. _____

Mark Blaine had waited years for a **promotion**. Finally, a week ago, he was offered the position he had always wanted – Regional Manager. On the same day, however, he won $6 million in the lottery. Mark's wife wants him to **resign** from his job and take her on a trip around the world. Mark says he cannot decide what to do.

B Look at the words in bold in the articles. What do you think they mean?

remote _____   skip _____   promotion _____

mainland _____   remarkably _____   resign _____

8 Complete the sentences. Use the simple past, the past continuous, or the past perfect of the verbs given.

1. In 2011, two divers _____*discovered*_____ (discover) the remains of a 200-year-old shipwreck while they _____ (dive) off the coast of Rhode Island, in the eastern United States.

2. After an art show _____ (open) in New York, it was discovered that someone _____ (hang) a famous painting by Henri Matisse upside down.

3. In 2015, workers _____ (find) a chemistry lab from the 1840s while they _____ (repair) a building at the University of Virginia in the United States. The lab was behind a wall of the current building.

4. Chile's Calbuco volcano _____ (surprise) residents of Santiago when it erupted in 2015. Before that, an eruption of Calbuco _____ (not happen) for over 40 years.

9 Read this situation. Then use the information and clues to complete the chart. Write the name of each reporter and each country. (You will leave one square in the chart blank.)

Ms. Johnson

Ms. Marshall

Mr. James

Mr. Grant

Mr. Simpson

Five news reporters – two women and three men – arrived for an international conference on Sunday, Monday, and Tuesday.

No more than two people came on the same day. The reporters came from five different countries.

Clues

The women: Ms. Johnson and Ms. Marshall

The men: Mr. James, Mr. Grant, and Mr. Simpson

The countries: Australia, Mexico, Brazil, Singapore, and the United States

The arrivals:

- Mr. Simpson arrived late at night. No one else had arrived that day.
- Ms. Johnson and Mr. Grant arrived on the same day.
- The man who came from Singapore had arrived the day before.
- The reporters who came from Brazil and Australia arrived on the same day.
- Mr. James and the woman who came from Brazil arrived on Tuesday, after Mr. Grant.
- The reporter from Australia arrived the day after the person who came from the United States.
- Mr. Grant came from North America but not the United States.

Reporters' countries and arrival days			
Sunday	Name: _____	Name: _____	
	Country: _____	Country: _____	
Monday	Name: _____	Name: _____	
	Country: _____	Country: _____	
Tuesday	Name: _____	Name: _____	
	Country: _____	Country: _____	

5 Expanding your horizons

1 Complete these sentences. Use words from the box.

☐ confident ☐ depressed ☐ fascinated ☐ uncomfortable
☐ curious ☑ embarrassed ☐ uncertain ☐ worried

1. In my country, people never leave tips. So when I first went abroad, I kept forgetting to tip servers. I felt really __embarrassed__.

2. The first time I traveled abroad, I felt really _____. I was alone, I didn't speak the language, and I didn't make any friends.

3. I just spent a year in France learning to speak French. It was a satisfying experience, and I was _____ by the culture.

4. At first I really didn't like shopping in the open-air markets. I felt _____ because so many people were trying to sell me something at the same time.

5. When I arrived in Lisbon, I was nervous because I couldn't speak any Portuguese. As I began to learn the language, though, I became more _____ about living there.

6. Before I went to Alaska last winter, I was very _____ about the cold. But it wasn't a problem because most buildings there are well heated.

7. When I was traveling in Southeast Asia, I couldn't believe how many different kinds of fruit there were. I was _____ to try all of them, so I ate a lot of fruit!

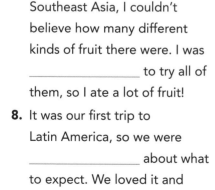

8. It was our first trip to Latin America, so we were _____ about what to expect. We loved it and hope to return again soon.

2 Imagine you are going to travel to a country you have never visited before. Write sentences using the factors and feelings given. Then add another sentence explaining your feelings.

Factors	Feelings
public transportation	anxious (about)
shopping	comfortable (with)
the climate	curious (about)
the food	enthusiastic (about)
the language	fascinated (by)
the money	nervous (about)
the music	uncertain (about)
the people my age	uncomfortable (with)

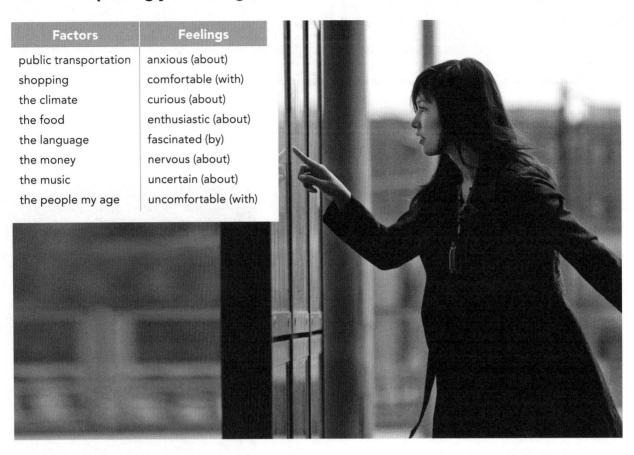

1. Public transportation is something I'd be anxious about. I'd be afraid of getting lost.

2.

3.

4.

5.

6.

7.

8.

9.

3 **Culture shock!**

A Make a list of four pieces of advice to help people feel comfortable about traveling abroad.

B Scan the article about cultural differences. Where can you find articles like this? Who was it written for?

Culture Shock

Each society has its own beliefs, attitudes, customs, behaviors, and social habits. These things give people a sense of who they are and how they are supposed to behave.

People become conscious of such rules when they meet people from different cultures. For example, the rules about when to eat vary from culture to culture. Many North Americans and Europeans organize their timetables around three mealtimes a day. In other countries, however, it's not the custom to have strict rules like this – people eat when they want to, and every family has its own timetable.

When people visit or live in a country for the first time, they are often surprised at the differences between this culture and the culture in their own country. For some people, traveling abroad is the thing they enjoy most in life; for others, cultural differences make them feel uncomfortable, frightened, and insecure. This is known as "culture shock."

When you're visiting a foreign country, it is important to understand and appreciate cultural differences. This can help you avoid misunderstandings, develop friendships more easily, and feel more comfortable when traveling or living abroad.

Here are several things to do in order to avoid culture shock.

1 Instead of criticizing, enjoy the new customs you discover each day on your trip as much as possible.

2 If you read or understand the language, read a local newspaper or listen to the radio to find out what news they're likely to be talking about.

3 Talk to people in order to understand their ideas about their own country as well as their thoughts about yours.

4 Remember the proverb, "When in Rome, do as the Romans do." It's a great way to start learning new things!

5 For instance, try one new thing every day, like a food you've never had before, instead of choosing something on the menu that you can have in your own country.

6 Read a book about the history of the place you are in so you will understand it better while you are there.

7 Go to concerts, museums, theatrical performances, and sporting events to appreciate the culture of this country.

8 Remember that traveling is an educational experience, so be ready to question the stereotypes you may have of another country, and learn about the stereotypes people in that country may have about the place you come from.

C Read the article. Use your own words to write definitions for these words.

1. culture _____

2. culture shock _____

3. appreciate _____

4. stereotypes _____

D After reading the article, would you make any changes to the pieces of advice you listed in part A?

4 **Complete these sentences by giving information about customs in a country you know.**

1. If you go for a long ride in a friend's car, <u>*it's the custom to offer to pay for some of the expenses.*</u>

2. When a friend graduates from school or college, _____

_____

3. If you borrow something from a friend, _____

_____

4. When a friend invites you to dinner, _____

_____

5 **Contrasting customs**

A Read the information about the different customs and find four pairs of countries with contrasting customs. Write the countries on the lines below.

Country	Custom
Brazil	Friends kiss each other three or four times on the cheeks as a greeting.
Denmark	People generally arrive on time for most occasions.
Egypt	People allow their hosts to treat them to meals in restaurants.
France	Service is usually included in the price of a meal in restaurants.
Japan	People bow when they see or meet someone they know.
New Zealand	People usually pay for their own meals in restaurants.
Spain	People usually arrive late for most appointments.
United States	People leave a tip of 15–20 percent in restaurants.

1. <u>Brazil and Japan</u>   **3.** _____

2. _____   **4.** _____

B Read these five cross-cultural situations. Write sentences describing what the visitors did wrong. Use the expressions in the box.

| you're (not) supposed to |
| you're (not) expected to |
| it's (not) the custom to |
| it's (not) acceptable to |

1. Enni is from Denmark. When she was on vacation in Spain, some Spanish friends invited her to dinner at 9:00. She arrived at exactly 9:00, but her friends had not even arrived home yet.

   In Spain, you're expected to _____

   _____

2. Kayla is from the United States. During her first week in Paris, she went to a restaurant with some new friends. She was so happy with the service that she left a tip of 20 percent. Her friends were a little embarrassed.

   In France, _____

   _____

3. James is from New Zealand. When he went to Egypt, he was invited to dinner at a restaurant. When the bill came, he offered to pay for his dinner. His Egyptian friend was kind of upset.

   In Egypt, _____

   _____

4. Clara is from Brazil. She was working for a year in Osaka, Japan. One day, when she saw a Japanese co-worker in a bookstore, she went to say hello and kissed him on the cheeks. Her friend was very surprised.

   _____

   _____

5. Brian is from Canada. He was on vacation in Bali, Indonesia, and some new friends invited him to a temple to watch a special dance performance. He arrived on time wearing a clean T-shirt and shorts, but they said he couldn't go inside the temple because he wasn't dressed properly.

   _____

   _____

6 **Complete these sentences with information about yourself (1–4)
and about a country you know well (5–8).**

1. One reason I'd feel homesick abroad is _____

2. Something that would fascinate me would be _____

3. Traveling alone is something _____

4. Getting used to hot weather is one thing _____

5. In _____, it's the custom to _____

6. If you have good service in a restaurant, _____

7. You're expected to _____ when _____

8. It's just not acceptable to _____ if _____

7 **Write about living in a foreign country. In the first paragraph, write
about two things you would enjoy. In the second paragraph, write
about two things you might worry about.**

If I lived in Colombia, I'd enjoy learning about the music scene – the local bands and singers who are popular there. Another thing I'd be fascinated by is . . . However, one thing that I'd be nervous about is the food. It might be very different from what I know. Something else I might be uncomfortable with is . . .

That needs fixing.

1 What's wrong with it?

A What can be wrong with these things? Put these words in the correct categories.
(Most words go in more than one category.)

| bike | blouse | car | carpet | chair | glasses | plate | sink | tablecloth |

chipped	cracked	dented	leaking	scratched	stained	torn

B What is wrong with these things? Use the words in part A to write a sentence about each one.

1. _The car is scratched._ OR
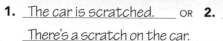
There's a scratch on the car.

2. _____

_____

3. _____

_____

4. _____

_____

5. _____

_____

6. _____

_____

7. _____

_____

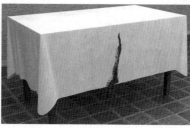

8. _____

_____

9. _____

_____

2 Problems, problems, problems!

A Scan the articles in *Consumer* magazine. Who would read articles like these? Why?

George's Class Trip

George Humphrey is a Spanish teacher at Crockett College in Duluth, Minnesota. Last year, George took his summer class from Duluth to Madrid, Spain. At the end of the six-week trip, George and the twenty students had a delayed flight at the airport in Madrid when they were coming home. Because of the six-hour delay in Madrid, they missed their plane from New York to Minnesota. Everyone had to stay at a hotel in New York City, and they all spent a lot more money than they had expected. They were also more than 24 hours late when they finally got back to Duluth. When George asked the airline office in New York to pay for their hotel and restaurant bills, the airline refused.

George contacted *Consumer* magazine. We talked to a representative of the airline office in Madrid and discovered that, in Europe, airlines must pay for delays – but that does not apply to airlines in the U.S. However, because the delay first occurred in Madrid, George and each student received 400 euros. George was very pleased, especially for his students. In his email to us, George wrote that he believes the law regarding airline delays needs changing in the U.S.

Diane's Vacation

Diane Gleason is a clothing designer in Cincinnati, Ohio. For her vacation last year, she decided to go somewhere she had never been – the southwestern part of the U.S. When she arrived at the airport in Phoenix, Arizona, she rented a beautiful red convertible for her trip. She planned to drive from Phoenix to the Grand Canyon to go hiking with friends for a few days. After she left the airport, Diane spent the night in Phoenix. The next morning, Diane discovered that someone had stolen the car from the parking lot. She called the car-rental agency, and they told her she was responsible for the cost of the car because she had left the keys in it. They would not let her rent another car until she paid for the stolen one. Diane didn't know what to do. She went back to the motel and contacted *Consumer* magazine.

We called the rental agency, and they told us that Diane had not bought special insurance for a stolen car. We told the agency that Diane needed help: she was all alone and feeling worried and depressed about what happened. The agency suggested that we contact Diane's credit card company. We did, and they told us that Diane was protected because of her credit card. They would pay for the stolen car! By evening, Diane had rented another car from the same agency and, that night, she had dinner at the Grand Canyon with her friends.

B Read the articles and complete the chart. Did George and Diane receive money?

	Problems	What *Consumer* magazine did	Received money? Yes	No
1. George's trip	delay in Madrid		☐	☐
2. Diane's vacation			☐	☐

3 **Choose appropriate verbs to complete the sentences. Use passive infinitives (*to be* + past participle) or gerunds.**

> **Language note: Verbs ending in *-en* or *-n***
>
> Some verbs are formed by adding *-en* or *-n* to a noun or adjective.
>
> These verbs mean "to make more of something."
>
> | Noun | | Verb | Adjective | | Verb |
> |------|---|------|-----------|---|------|
> | length | → | length**en** | loose | → | loose**n** |
> | (make something longer) | | | (make something looser) | | |

  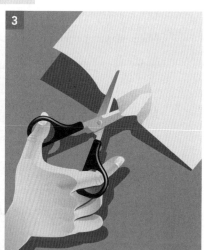

☑ lengthen ☐ loosen ☐ sharpen ☐ shorten ☐ tighten ☐ widen

1. This jacket is too short.

_It needs to be lengthened._____ OR

_It needs lengthening._____

2. The screws on these glasses are too loose.

They need _____

3. The blades on these scissors are too dull.

They need _____

4. This faucet is too tight.

It needs _____

5. These pants are too long.

They need _____

6. This street is too narrow.

It needs _____

4 Complete the conversation. Use *keep, keeps, need,* or *needs* with passive infinitives or gerunds of the verbs given.

Jack: Guess what? Someone broke into my car last night!

Mia: Oh, no. What did they take?

Jack: Nothing! But they did a lot of damage. The lock
needs to be repaired (repair). And
the window _____
(replace).

Mia: It was probably some young kids having "fun."

Jack: Yeah, some fun. I think they had a party in my car! The seats
_____ (clean).

Mia: How annoying. Does the car drive OK?

Jack: No, it feels strange. The gears _____
(stick), so they _____ (fix). And the brakes
_____ (check) right away.

Mia: Well, I guess you're lucky they didn't steal it!

Jack: Yeah, lucky me.

5 Write about something you bought that had something wrong with it. In the first paragraph, describe the problem. In the second paragraph, explain what you did about it.

Recently, I bought an espresso machine. While I was unpacking it, I could see it was already damaged. The glass carafe was chipped and needed to be replaced. And to make matters worse, the machine leaked!
I took it back to the store. I was worried because the machine had been on sale, and I had lost my receipt. Luckily, the clerk didn't ask me for it. She said a lot of customers had recently had the same problem, and she gave me a better machine at the same price.

_____

_____

_____

_____

_____

_____

_____

_____

6 Paul will fix it!

A Match each problem with the repair needed.

PAUL'S REPAIR SHOP

ITEM	PROBLEM	REPAIR NEEDED
1. dishwasher	doesn't work ___f___	a. tighten and glue the legs
2. DVD player	DVD is stuck _____	b. repair the wire
3. speakers	wire is damaged _____	c. remove the DVD
4. dresser	mirror is cracked _____	d. repaint the door
5. stove	metal door is scratched _____	e. replace the mirror
6. table	legs are loose _____	f. check the motor

B Write a sentence describing each problem. Then add a sentence describing the action needed to fix it. Use passive infinitives or gerunds.

1. _The dishwasher doesn't work. The motor needs to be checked._ OR
   The motor needs checking.

2. _____

3. _____

4. _____

5. _____

6. _____

C Think of three items you own that are damaged (or were damaged) in some way. Write a sentence describing each problem. Then write another sentence describing the action needed to fix it.

1. _____

2. _____

3. _____

7 Complete the sentences with the correct forms of the words in the box.

☐ chip	☑ drop	☐ freeze	☐ scratch
☐ clean	☐ fix	☐ jam	☐ stick
☐ die	☐ flicker	☐ leak	☐ torn

1. This cell phone is driving me crazy! My calls keep ___*dropping*___ .

2. Your computer screen is so dirty. It needs to be _____ .

3. Something is wrong with your TV screen. It keeps _____ . It's time to get a new one.

4. I hate this printer. It keeps _____ . The copies won't come out.

5. Be careful – your cup is _____ . I don't want you to cut yourself.

6. The buttons on this remote control keep _____ . Do you have something to clean it with?

7. Do you realize your jeans are _____ in the back?

8. Your bathroom faucet keeps _____ . Do you want me to try to fix it?

9. My new glasses already have a _____ on one of the lenses. How did that happen?

10. Did your laptop _____ again? I find that so annoying.

11. This old scanner doesn't work at all anymore. It needs to be _____ .

12. The battery in my cell phone keeps _____ . I should buy a new one.

7 What can we do?

1 **Use the information in the pamphlet and the verbs and prepositions given below to change the sentences from the active to the passive.**

HERE ARE JUST SOME OF THE DANGERS FACING YOU AND YOUR CHILDREN.

The water we drink

1. Agricultural runoff is contaminating the water supply.
2. Chlorine and other additives have ruined the taste of our drinking water.

The food we eat

3. Certain agricultural pesticides have caused new illnesses.
4. Pollution from cars and trucks is destroying our crops.

The air we breathe

5. Factories are releasing dangerous chemicals.
6. Breathing smog every day has damaged many people's health.

The world we live in

7. The lack of rainfall has created more severe droughts.
8. Global warming is threatening our forests and wildlife.

Join **Save Our Planet** today!

1. <u>The water supply is being contaminated due to agricultural runoff.</u> (due to)
2. _____ (by)
3. _____ (by)
4. _____ (because of)
5. _____ (by)
6. _____ (as a result of)
7. _____ (through)
8. _____ (by)

2 Verbs and nouns

A Complete the chart.

Verb	Noun	Verb	Noun
contaminate	contamination	educate	_____
contribute	_____	_____	pollution
_____	creation	populate	_____
deplete	_____	protect	_____
_____	destruction	_____	reduction

B Write four sentences like the ones in Exercise 1 using words from the chart.

Example: _Many rivers and streams have been badly contaminated by industrial waste._

1. _____
2. _____
3. _____
4. _____

3 Choose the correct words or phrases.

El Yunque rain forest

1. Green organizations are trying to save rain forests that have been ___threatened___ by developers and farmers. (created / ruined / threatened)

2. One way to inform the public about factories that pollute the environment is through _____ programs on TV. (agricultural / educational / industrial)

3. In many countries around the world, threatened animal and plant species are being _____ by strict laws. (created / polluted / protected)

4. Agricultural pesticides are _____ the soil in many countries. (damaging / eating up / lowering)

5. _____ is an enormous problem in many large cities where whole families can only afford to live in one room. (pollution / poverty / waste)

4 How safe is the fleece you are wearing?

A Scan the title and first two paragraphs of this article. What is fleece?
Do you own clothing made of fleece? What clothing?

The Fleece that Came to Dinner

Today, half of the clothing bought by people is made of a synthetic fiber. And that figure is almost 70% in the developing world. Synthetics – or fibers that are created by science, not by nature – are very attractive to customers because, for example, some of them are water-resistant, which is particularly desirable for rain gear and hiking shoes. Moreover, synthetics don't require the amount of water, labor, and land that is needed to cultivate cotton and other natural fibers.

One of the most popular synthetic fabrics is called fleece, a name that originally referred to the wool from a sheep, which is still used to make fall and winter clothes. But in the twenty-first century, the word "fleece" refers to the inexpensive, lightweight, and often water-resistant synthetic material that more and more people are wearing today.

One of the most interesting things about fleece is the fact that it can be made from recycled plastic bottles. This means that fleece can be far less expensive than wool or other natural fibers. For many people, recycling plastic bottles is thought of as friendly to the natural environment since we are reusing the plastic, not burying it in the ground or dumping it in the oceans. However, in the last few years, scientists have discovered that fleece may not be as environmentally friendly as we once supposed.

Scientists are now finding very small particles of plastic at the bottom of the ocean that they believe are the remains of fleece that is washed in washing machines every day all over the world. When it is washed, more than 1,500 particles may separate from a fleece product into the water. When that water is drained, some of it will make its way back into the lakes, rivers, and oceans of our world. That is what seems to be happening now. When the synthetic particles reach natural bodies of water, the plastic is going to be eaten by fish because it looks like food to them. And sooner or later, those fish are going to be caught, delivered to the food market, and end up on your plate at dinner.

What can be done? Shall we return to more costly, heavier, and traditional natural fibers such as cotton and wool? Are people willing to spend more money to possibly save the environment? Or is economics so important to people who have very little money that they believe they cannot afford to give up their synthetic fibers?

B Read the article. Check (✓) the true statements. For statements that are false, write the true information.

1. ☐ In the developing world, 50% of people buy clothing made of synthetic fiber.

_____

2. ☐ The word "fleece" originally meant sheep's wool.

_____

3. ☐ Fleece is made from recycled plastic bottles.

_____

4. ☐ More than 2,000 particles of fleece may separate during washing.

_____

5. ☐ Fortunately, fish will not consume particles of fleece.

_____

6. ☐ We now know that people are going to stop using fleece because of its dangers.

_____

5 World issues

A Match the nouns and definitions.

Nouns	Definitions
1. infectious diseases ___d___	**a.** physical actions that are meant to cause destruction or injury
2. global warming _____	**b.** a period of time when businesses are not doing well and a large number of people cannot find jobs
3. government corruption _____	**c.** an extreme lack of money
4. famine _____	**d.** illnesses that can be passed on to other people
5. political unrest _____	**e.** a situation in which people do not have enough food
6. poverty _____	**f.** a situation in which citizens become angry or violent due to their dissatisfaction with their government
7. recession _____	**g.** illegal or dishonest activity by people with political power
8. violence _____	**h.** a situation in which a number of people are not working because they cannot find jobs
9. unemployment _____	**i.** an increase in the world's average temperatures

B Choose the correct noun from part A to complete each sentence. You will not use all of the words.

1. It seems like there are more dangerous _____ these days, like swine flu and the Zika virus.

2. During the recent _____, 30 percent of the businesses in my town closed, and a large part of the population didn't have jobs.

3. There's so much _____ in this city. I'm afraid to walk on the streets alone at night because I don't feel safe.

4. Before you travel to a foreign country, make sure there are no dangerous political situations going on there. It can be unsafe to visit countries that are experiencing _____.

5. In the 1800s, a large portion of Irish potato crops were destroyed by disease. Because potatoes were a major part of the Irish diet, there was a major _____ and over 1.5 million people died.

6. People in this country don't trust the police or city officials because there is a lot of _____.

6 Complete the conversations. Use the expressions in the box and the information in the list.

One thing to do . . .	The best way to fight . . .
Another thing to do . . .	One way to help . . .

- [✓] complain to the Parks Department about it
- [ ] create more government-funded jobs
- [ ] create more public housing projects
- [ ] organize a public meeting to protest the threat of public property
- [ ] educate young people about its dangers
- [ ] report it to the local newspaper
- [ ] donate money to charities that provide shelters and food

A new housing development?

1. A: A big housing developer wants to build an apartment complex in Forest Hill Park. I think that's terrible, but what can we do?

B: _One thing to do is to complain to the Parks Department about it._

A: That's a good idea.

B: _____

2. A: Personally, I'm worried about violence in the city. The streets are not safe at night.

B: _____

3. A: You know, there's a lot of corruption in our city government.

B: _____

A: Yeah, the bad publicity might help to clean things up a bit.

4. A: There are so many unemployed people in this city. I just don't know what can be done about it.

B: _____

5. A: What worries me most is the number of homeless people on the streets.

B: _____

A: I agree.

B: _____

7 **Complete the sentences using the present continuous passive or the present perfect passive. Then suggest a solution to each problem.**

1. A lot of jobs _____have been lost_____ (lose) in recent years.

   One way to deal with unemployment ___is to bring more businesses___ into the area.

2. These days, a lot of endangered animals _____ (kill) by hunters and poachers.

   The best way to stop this practice _____

   _____.

3. During the past few years, lots of trees _____ (destroy) by acid rain.

   One thing to do about it _____

   _____.

4. Underground water _____ (contaminate) by agricultural pesticides.

   The best way to deal with the problem _____

   _____.

5. Too many people _____ (affect) by infectious diseases in the past few years.

   The best way to stop this _____

   _____.

8 **Write two paragraphs about a charity, an organization that helps people. In the first paragraph, describe what the charity does. In the second paragraph, explain why you think the charity is useful.**

A good charity in my city is Shelter. This organization works to reduce the number of homeless people on our streets. Shelter believes the best way to do this is to . . .

Shelter is my favorite charity because homelessness is, in my opinion, the greatest problem facing my city. Many people cannot find jobs, and . . .

_____

_____

_____

_____

_____

_____

_____

_____

8 Never stop learning.

1 Choose the correct words or phrases.

1. I'm interested in human behavior, so I'm planning to take a class in _____.
   (geography / psychology / math)

2. I want to take a course in _____, such as commerce or accounting.
   (education / business / social science)

3. I'd prefer not to study _____ because I'm not very comfortable in hospitals. (engineering / new media / nursing)

4. I'd really like to work in Information Technology, so I'm thinking of taking courses in _____.
   (computer science / finance / English)

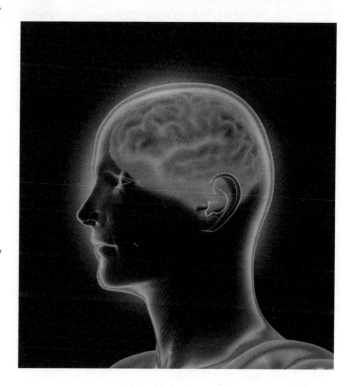

2 What would you prefer?

A Write questions with *would rather* or *would prefer* using the cues.

1. take a science class / an art class

   Would you rather take a science class or an art class?_____ OR

   Would you prefer to take a science class or an art class?_____

2. study part time / full time

   _____

3. have a boring job that pays well / an exciting job that pays less

   _____

4. take a long vacation once a year / several short vacations each year

   _____

B Write answers to the questions in part A.

1. _____
2. _____
3. _____
4. _____

3 Love it or leave it

A First, complete speaker A's questions with four things you would not like to do. Use ideas in the box or your own ideas.

> learn to play the accordion
> learn clothing design
> learn how to repair watches
> study sociology
> take a class in personal finance
> take a cooking class

1. **A:** _Do you want to learn to play the accordion?_
   B: _I'd rather not. I'd prefer to learn to play the piano._   OR
   I'd prefer not to. I'd rather learn to play the piano.

2. **A:** Do you want to _____?
   B: _____

3. **A:** Would you like to _____?
   B: _____

4. **A:** Do you want to _____?
   B: _____

5. **A:** Would you like to _____?
   B: _____

B Now write responses for speaker B. Use the short answers *I'd rather not* or *I'd prefer not to* and say what you would prefer to do.

4 Answer these questions and give reasons.

1. On your day off, would you rather stay home or go out?
   I'd rather stay home than go out because _____

2. Would you prefer to have a cat or a bird?
   _____

3. Would you rather live in the city or the country?
   _____

4. When you entertain friends, would you rather invite them over for dinner
   or take them out to a restaurant?
   _____

5. Would you prefer to see a new movie at the theater or download it and watch it at home?
   _____

5 Online learning, the schools of the future?

A Have you taken an online class? Would you like to? Would you prefer to study online rather than at school? Write your answers.

_____

_____

B Read the online newspaper article. Underline the sentences that contain the answers to these questions.

1. What is a MOOC?

2. Why do so few students complete a MOOC?

3. Do professors who teach MOOCs think that they are as difficult as courses taken in a classroom?

4. What are critics of MOOCs afraid of?

FREE COLLEGE FOR EVERYONE?
posted 21st of August

A revolution in education is going to happen. Massive Online Open Courses (MOOCs for short) are designed for students who cannot afford, cannot get to, or simply don't want to attend classes in a university classroom. MOOCs are going to be of great importance to economically disadvantaged people, as well as people who live far from a university campus. The only requirement to attend a MOOC is access to a computer with an Internet connection, which is becoming more common each day.

Many MOOCs are created by top professors in their fields who teach at prestigious universities in the U.S., like Princeton, Harvard, and Stanford. These professors may teach online courses at their universities, but with a MOOC they can reach students all over the world. At the moment, not all universities accept academic credit for a MOOC. However, almost half of the professors who have taught a MOOC believe that the coursework is as demanding as the work done in a traditional university class. Many of these professors are not paid for teaching MOOCs by their universities; they do it because they want to

make education available to everyone, they love teaching, and they enjoy being able to communicate with so many students online.

MOOC students do not pay tuition, which is perhaps the greatest appeal of these courses. Most professors do not even require students to buy textbooks, which can be very expensive as well. This further reduces the cost of education. On the other hand, despite the affordability of MOOCs, MOOC students do not receive diplomas, which may lessen their appeal. Students may receive certification if they

pass the course, but of the 33,000 students enrolled in MOOCs today, the completion rate is strikingly low, at only 10%. Because a MOOC doesn't cost anything, students don't have to worry about losing money if they decide to drop the class. And many of them ultimately do.

So while there are upsides to MOOCs, they are not without their critics. Some professors fear that in the future there may be two kinds of university courses: expensive and superior courses at a traditional university where small groups of students meet in classes with their professors, and inexpensive and inferior massive online courses where students will never meet their professors nor even their fellow students. These critics also point out that students must be disciplined self-starters to be successful in a MOOC and that students often develop the skills of perseverance, time-management, and self-discipline by learning together with other students in a traditional university classroom.

C Write answers to these questions.

1. Do you think MOOCs are going to be the courses of the future? Why or why not?

_____

_____

2. What do you see as the main advantage of MOOCs? The main disadvantage?

_____

_____

D What would you prefer to take as a MOOC: a humanities course (such as literature, art, or history) or a science course (such as biology, chemistry, or engineering)? Why did you choose that course?

6 Complete the sentences with *by* + gerund. Use *not* if needed. Use the ideas in the box or your own information.

cook at home	eat out	go out more often	study dance
eat good food	exercise regularly	stay home	use social media

cook at home

study dance

use social media

1. A good way to enjoy the weekend is <u>not by staying home but by going out with friends.</u>

2. A good way to keep in touch with old friends is _____

3. You can make new friends _____

4. The best way to save money is _____

5. You could stay in shape _____

6. I stay healthy _____

7. One way to learn self-confidence is _____

7 Choose the correct words or phrases.

1. Robin shows her _____ by volunteering to help people with cancer. (competitiveness / communication skills / concern for others)

2. When I was young, I didn't understand the importance of _____. But when I started paying my own bills, I realized it's an important skill. (money management / cooperation / perseverance)

3. I learned _____ from my parents. They taught me the importance of using my imagination and making art. (creativity / courtesy / self-confidence)

4. Gina always gets upset with people who disagree with her. I wish she would show more _____. (perseverance / self-confidence / tolerance)

5. I recently joined a choir, and I love it. But you need a lot of _____, because you have to practice the same piece of music for weeks before you're ready to perform it! (cooperation / perseverance / time management)

8 Personal qualities

A Read about each student in these descriptions and choose a suitable quality for each one.

☐ competitiveness ☐ creativity ☐ self-confidence ☐ time management
☐ cooperation ☐ perseverance ☐ self-discipline ☐ tolerance

1. Alex is always on time for everything. He's never even five minutes late. He keeps track of everything on his calendar. I wish I were as good at _____ as Alex is.

2. Frank finds school very hard, but no one tries harder than he does. He always spends the whole weekend at the library trying to keep up with his studies. He shows great

_____.

3. Melissa always wants to do better than everyone else. In school, she always tries to get the best grades. Her favorite sport is field hockey because she's the best player in the school. No one needs to teach Melissa _____.

4. Jennifer has more _____ than any of her classmates. She writes fascinating stories that show she has a wonderful imagination. She's also very artistic and does very interesting paintings.

B Write two similar descriptions of people you know. Either use two of the qualities you didn't use in part A or choose other qualities.

1. _____

_____

_____

_____

2. _____

_____

_____

_____

9 My way

A List two methods of learning each of these skills.

1. become a good guitarist
   <u>by teaching myself</u>
   <u>by taking lessons</u>

2. improve my writing ability in English
   _____
   _____

3. become a more confident public speaker
   _____
   _____

4. learn more about personal finance
   _____
   _____

5. become skilled at auto repair
   _____
   _____

6. learn a new computer program
   _____
   _____

my first guitar

15 years later

B Which of the two methods in part A would you prefer to use to develop each skill? Write sentences using *would rather (not)* or *would prefer (not)*. Give reasons.

1. <u>I'd rather learn guitar by teaching myself than by taking lessons.</u>
   <u>I'd prefer not to take lessons because they're expensive.</u>

2. _____

3. _____

4. _____

5. _____

6. _____

Getting things done

1 **Which service does each person need? Choose the correct word or phrase.**

☐ computer repair ☐ house painting
☐ dry cleaning ☐ language tutoring
☐ home repairs ☑ lawn mowing

1. _____ lawn mowing _____

Ken: I have a new home and don't have much time for yard work. I mowed the lawn two weeks ago, and I need to cut it again. I'd like to save money, but perhaps I'll just have to pay someone to do it for me.

2. _____

Akiko: I don't like the flowered wallpaper in my bedroom or the dark color of the walls in my living room. I want to have the wallpaper removed so the whole place looks bigger and brighter with fun, modern colors everywhere.

3. _____

Margaret: Now that it's getting colder, I need to take my winter clothes out of storage. Some things I can wash in the washing machine, but I should take my wool coat to that new place around the corner.

4. _____

Steven: I have a lot of work to do this week, but my laptop stopped working! I tried to fix it, but I don't know how. I can't afford to buy a new laptop.

5. _____

Eric: I'm so excited! I'm finally going to Quebec this summer. I studied French in high school, but I'm not sure how much I remember now. Do you know anyone who can help me improve my French?

6. _____

Karen: I really want to move into that studio apartment I found downtown. The only problem is that there are a lot of little things that need to be repaired. Where can I get a leaky faucet and a broken lock repaired?

home repairs

language tutoring

lawn mowing

2 Where can I get . . . ?

A Match the verbs in column A with the nouns in column B.

A	B	
cut	a stain	1. _____cut my hair_____
check	my blood pressure	2. _____
do	my computer	3. _____
fix	my hair	4. _____
print	my nails	5. _____
remove	my pants	6. _____
shorten	my photos	7. _____

B First, use the items in part A to write *Where can I get . . . ?* or *Where can I have . . . ?* questions for speaker A. Then write responses for speaker B using your own ideas.

1. **A:** _Where can I get my hair cut?_
   B: _You can get it cut at May's Salon._

2. **A:** _____

   B: _____

3. **A:** _____

   B: _____

4. **A:** _____

   B: _____

5. **A:** _____

   B: _____

6. **A:** _____

   B: _____

7. **A:** _____

   B: _____

3 **Where can you have these services done? Write sentences with *You can have . . . .***

Come to
SALON 21
for an
AMAZING
haircut!

1. *You can have your hair cut at Salon 21.*
_____

At **KWIK FIX**
we repair all kinds
of shoes.

2. _____
_____

**DREAM
CLEAN**
We dry-clean
your clothes
like no
one else.

3. _____
_____

**CARPET
WORLD**
*We'll clean your
carpets so they're
as good as new.*

4. _____
_____

We do nails (and only nails)
at **Nail File.**

5. _____
_____

JIMMY'S...

...the best
car wash in town!

*Service your
washing machine
to keep it running
its best.*
**Call Hal's Repairs
at 555-1838**

7. _____
_____

At **EYE to EYE,**

we can examine your eyes
in 30 minutes.

6. _____
_____

8. _____
_____

4 Less could be better

A Look at the two pictures. Where have you dreamed about living, in an apartment in the city or in a house in the suburbs? Why? Where would your parents like to live? Why?

DOWNSIZING

Do you want your parents' furniture, family photos, old toys, and sports equipment? If you're a millennial, the answer is likely to be "no."

Millennials are people who became adults at the beginning of the 21st century, and they are not necessarily interested in collecting things. And boomers, Americans born in the years after World War II, are finding out that their children have very different ideas about how to live "the good life."

Millennials do not feel the need to have a lot of *things*. They would rather have *experiences*, like tourism, art, and sports activities. This preference for "less is better" – or downsizing – is partly a result of the world economic crisis and the student debt that many young adults have. The lack of jobs has made millennials want to lower their expenses. And they feel that they must pay off their student loans before they can get married and have children of their own.

Because millennials are waiting to start families, they tend to prefer to live in apartments rather than large houses like their parents. First, they simply don't need that much space. Second, houses are expensive. Third, houses are often located in the suburbs, farther away from the culture and diversity that cities have to offer and that many millennials want.

But, in the latest twist of generational clashes, millennials are finding it more and more difficult to afford city living. Boomers, who generally have more money to spend than millennials, are finally ready to sell their houses now that their children have moved out. When they do, many then use that money to buy an apartment in the city where they can start a new life with all the amenities cities have to offer to people with money.

With this increase in demand, the prices of apartments have gone up, and millennials are discovering that it is very difficult to compete economically with their boomer parents. One option is for millennials to live together. Today some of them are renting houses or large apartments that several people can share. More than a few people think that this kind of downsizing, besides being good for the pocketbook, is good for the planet.

B Read the article about downsizing. Check (✓) the true statements.
For statements that are false, write the true information.

1. ☐ Adult children still enjoy receiving furniture from their parents.

2. ☐ Boomers are Americans born before World War II.

3. ☐ Downsizing is the philosophy that "less is better."

4. ☐ The competition between boomers and millennials has a lot to do with money.

5. ☐ The next step in downsizing could be for boomers and millennials to share houses and large apartments.

5 Write two suggestions for each of these problems.

1. **A:** I never have any energy, so I can never do anything except work. I sleep all weekend, so don't tell me to get more rest!

   B: Have you thought about <u>taking an aerobics class?</u>
   <u>Another option is to improve your diet.</u>

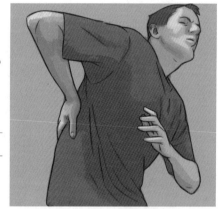

2. **A:** My problem is a constant backache. I just don't know what to do to get rid of it. I had someone give me a massage, but it didn't really help.

   B: Maybe you could _____

   _____

3. **A:** My doctor told me to get more exercise. She strongly recommended swimming, but I find swimming so boring! In fact, aren't all sports boring?

   B: Why don't you _____

   _____

4. **A:** I'm very sociable, and I have great difficulty saying no. I end up doing things every night of the week – going to parties, clubs, the movies. I'm so tired all the time!

   B: It might be a good idea _____

   _____

5. **A:** I like to be a good neighbor, but the woman next door drives me crazy. She's always knocking on my door to chat. And whenever I go out into the yard, she goes into her yard – and talks for hours!

   B: What about _____

   _____

6 Choose the correct three-word phrasal verb for each sentence.

1. I don't know how my grandmother _____ all the new technology. She's better at understanding new gadgets than I am! (comes up with / cuts down on / keeps up with)

2. My cousin didn't know what to do for her mother's 60th birthday, but she finally _____ the idea of a surprise picnic with the whole family. (came up with / got along with / looked forward to)

3. Ilene has done it again! She only met Chris two months ago, and already she has _____ him. Why doesn't she try to work out any problems? (broken up with / gotten along with / kept up with)

4. After Michelle saw her doctor, she decided to _____ eating fast food. She wants to lose some weight and start exercising again in order to keep fit. (cut down on / look forward to / take care of)

5. We're really lucky in my family because we all _____ each other very well. (come up with / get along with / look forward to)

6. I've done pretty badly in my classes this semester, so I'm not really _____ receiving my grades. (getting along with / looking forward to / taking care of)

7. I can't _____ that loud music anymore! I can't stand hip-hop, and I'm going to tell my neighbor right now. (cut down on / put up with / take care of)

8. I've been getting sick a lot lately, and I often feel tired. I really need to start _____ my health. (cutting down on / keeping up with / taking care of)

10 A matter of time

1 Circle the correct word that describes each sentence.

1. Events in December 2010 led to the peaceful removal of Tunisia's prime minister in January 2011. (natural disaster / epidemic / (revolution))

2. In 2014, a new species of insect was found in Vietnam. It has a body over 30 centimeters long and is the second longest insect in the world. (discovery / invention / epidemic)

3. On June 12, 2016, a gunman entered a nightclub in Florida where he killed 49 people and injured more than 50. (invention / terrorist act / achievement)

4. Advances in robot technology have come a long way in recent years. Scientists like Japan's Hiroshi Ishiguro have created human-like robots that can have conversations with each other and with humans. (achievement / disaster / terrorist act)

5. Prime Minister Benazir Bhutto of Pakistan was killed after leaving a campaign rally in December 2007. (assassination / election / revolution)

6. In 2010, a series of floods in Australia affected over 200,000 people and caused nearly a billion Australian dollars in damage. (discovery / natural disaster / epidemic)

2 Complete the sentences. Use words from the box.

ago	for	from	in	since	to

1. Jazz first became popular _____in_____ the 1920s.

2. The cell phone was invented about 45 years _____.

3. Brasília has been the capital city of Brazil _____ 1960.

4. The first laptop was produced _____ 1981.

5. Mexico has been independent _____ more than 200 years.

6. World War II lasted _____ 1939 _____ 1945.

7. Vietnam was separated into two parts _____ about 20 years.

8. East and West Germany have been united _____ 1990.

jazz

Brasília

3 Nouns and verbs

A Complete this chart. Then check your answers in a dictionary.

Noun	Verb	Noun	Verb
achievement	_achieve_	existence	_____
assassination	_____	exploration	_____
demonstration	_____	explosion	_____
discovery	_____	invention	_____
discrimination	_____	transformation	_____
election	_____	vaccination	_____

B Choose verbs from the chart in part A to complete these sentences. Use the correct verb tense.

Bangalore, a high-tech center

a research station in Antarctica

1. Over the past several decades, the Indian city of Bangalore has _transformed_ itself into a high-tech center.

2. In World War I, many soldiers were _____ against typhoid, a deadly bacterial disease.

3. Aung San, the man who led Myanmar to independence, was _____ in 1947. No one is certain who killed him.

4. The European Union has _____ since 1957.

5. Until the 1960s, there were many laws that _____ against African Americans in certain regions of the United States.

6. In 1885, Louis Pasteur _____ a cure for rabies when he treated a young boy who was bitten by a dog.

7. In recent years, teams of experts in countries such as Cambodia and Angola have been safely _____ land mines in order to rid those countries of these dangerous weapons.

8. One of the few parts of the world that has not been _____ much is Antarctica. The extreme climate makes it dangerous to travel far from research centers.

4 Vaccines past, present, and future

A What are vaccinations? If necessary, scan the article to find out.

VACCINATIONS

For well over a thousand years, smallpox was a disease that everyone feared. The disease killed much of the native population in South America when the Spanish arrived there in the early sixteenth century. By the end of the eighteenth century, smallpox was responsible for the deaths of about one in ten people around the world. Those who survived the disease were left with ugly scars on their skin.

It had long been well known among farmers that people who worked with cows rarely caught smallpox; instead, they often caught a similar but much milder disease called cowpox. A British doctor named Edward Jenner was fascinated by this, and so he studied cowpox. He became convinced that, by injecting people with cowpox, he could protect them against the much worse disease smallpox. In 1796, he vaccinated a boy with cowpox and, two months later, with smallpox. The boy did not get smallpox. In the next two years, Jenner vaccinated several children in the same way, and none of them got the disease.

News of Jenner's success soon spread. In 1800, the Royal Vaccine Institution was founded in Berlin, Germany. In the following year, Napoleon opened a similar institute in Paris, France. It took nearly two centuries to achieve Jenner's dream of ridding the world of smallpox. In 1967, the World Health Organization (WHO) started an ambitious vaccination program, and the last known case of smallpox was recorded in Somalia in 1977.

The future of vaccinations aims at the eradication of three diseases that can be caused by mosquito bites: malaria, Zika virus, and dengue. Malaria is an infectious disease that is still a problem, in part because the virus that causes the disease hides in the cells away from the immune system. Zika virus has recently been discovered in various places all over the world, and it is particularly dangerous for pregnant women. At this time there is no vaccine for Zika virus, although scientists are working on one. Dengue is a disease that has multiplied alarmingly in recent years, but in the last two years a vaccine has been successfully developed for people between 9 and 45 years old.

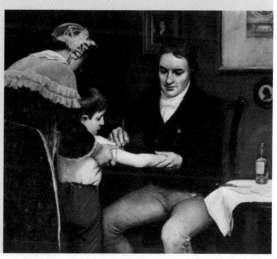

B Read the article about vaccinations. Complete the chart with the history of events in the story of vaccinations.

Date	Event
1. Early 16th century	Smallpox killed much of the native population in South America.
2. End of the 18th century	
3. 1796	
4. 1800	
5. 1801	
6. 1967	
7. 1977	
8. Future challenge	

5 Life in 2050

A Complete these predictions about life in 2050. Use the future continuous of the verb given. Then add two more predictions of your own.

Life on the moon?

By 2050, . . .

1. some people _____will be living_____ in cities on the moon. (live)

2. many people _____ temperature-controlled body suits. (wear)

3. most people _____ cars that run on fuel from garbage. (drive)

4. people _____ in a new Olympic event – mind reading. (compete)

5. _____
   _____

6. _____
   _____

B Complete these predictions about what will have happened by 2050. Use the future perfect. Then add two more predictions of your own.

By 2050, . . .

1. computers _____will have replaced_____ people as translators. (replace)

2. ties for men _____ out of fashion. (go)

3. scientists _____ a cheap way of getting drinking water from seawater. (discover)

4. medical researchers _____ a cure for cancer. (find)

5. _____
   _____

6. _____
   _____

A cure for cancer?

6 Write two responses to each question.

1. What will or won't you be doing in ten years? (Use the future continuous.)

   I won't be living with my parents.

   _____

   _____

2. How will cities of the future be different? (Use *will*.)

   Cities won't allow cars downtown.

   _____

   _____

3. How will life in small villages in your country have changed in the next 20 years?
   (Use the future perfect.)

   More people will have moved back from cities to small villages.

   _____

   _____

4. How do you think the world's weather will change during this century? (Use *will*.)

   The weather will be warmer, and the summers will be longer.

   _____

   _____

5. What advances will scientists have made by 2050? (Use the future perfect.)

   Scientists will have found a way to grow enough food for everyone.

   _____

   _____

7 Think of four more ways that technology will affect how we live and work in the next 20 years.

1. <u>Robots will be cleaning our homes.</u>

2. _____

   _____

3. _____

   _____

4. _____

   _____

5. _____

   _____

8 Write two paragraphs about one of these topics or a topic of your choice. In the first paragraph, describe the past. In the second paragraph, describe how you think the future will be.

| a music group | changes within a country | health |
| space exploration | changes within a region | technology |

Eyeglasses were invented in the 13th century in Italy. These early glasses didn't include earpieces to keep the glasses on the wearer's face. Instead, they had to be held in front of the eyes or placed on the nose. In the 1700s, eyeglasses were designed with earpieces, making them easier to use. In the 20th century, contacts became common, making it even easier and more convenient for people to use corrective lenses.

Technological advances have continued to make vision correction more practical and convenient. In recent years, doctors have developed laser surgery techniques, which can make corrective lenses unnecessary for people with certain types of vision problems. In the future, computer technology will probably replace eyeglasses, contact lenses, and laser surgery. It may even make it possible for blind people to see.

_____

_____

_____

_____

_____

_____

_____

11 Rites of passage

1 Milestones

A Read these statements. Check (✓) the ones that are true for you. For statements that are false, write the true information.

Example: As soon as I got my first cell phone, I called all my friends.

The moment I got a cell phone, I called my parents OR
I've never had a cell phone.

1. ☐ By the time I was three years old, I had already learned two languages.

_____

2. ☐ Before I started school, I was carefree – I used to watch TV all day.

_____

3. ☐ After I started taking the bus by myself, I became more independent.

_____

4. ☐ As soon as I got my driver's license, my parents let me drive everywhere.

_____

5. ☐ The moment I earned my own money, I opened a bank account.

_____

6. ☐ Once I started learning English, I quit studying other languages.

_____

7. ☐ Until I graduated from high school, I was very unsophisticated.

_____

8. ☐ Before I became more independent, I thought I knew more than my parents.

_____

B Write three true statements about how things have changed over time for you, your family, or your friends. Use time clauses.

1. _____

_____

2. _____

_____

3. _____

_____

2 Complete these descriptions. Use words from the box.

- ☐ ambitious
- ☐ argumentative
- ☐ carefree
- ☐ naive
- ☐ rebellious
- ☑ sophisticated

1. Sandra is so _____sophisticated_____. She always dresses well, she knows lots of intelligent people, and she never says anything silly.

2. I just spent a horrible evening with Patricia. She questioned and criticized everything I said. I wish she weren't so _____.

3. My sister is very _____. She trusts everyone and thinks everyone is good.

4. Once I turned 16, I became less _____, and my parents started to let me do what I wanted.

5. Eric is really _____. He wants to own his own business by the time he's 25.

6. I wish I could be like Susie. She's so _____ and never seems to worry about anything.

3 Do you have a friend who is special to you? Write about him or her. In the first paragraph, describe the person. In the second paragraph, describe a particular time when the person helped you.

One of my best friends is Jennifer. She's very mature and conscientious, and she always gives me good advice. Until I met her, I had been making some bad decisions . . . .

Jennifer is also very generous. She always helps her friends when they need it. For example, the moment she found out I was sick last winter, she came over and visited me.

_____

_____

_____

_____

_____

_____

_____

4 Turning points

A Scan the article from a sports magazine about Usain Bolt. What lesson did he learn as a child?

LEARNING FAST

Usain Bolt is called "Lightning" Bolt because he is considered the fastest man in the world. The Jamaican runner is an Olympic champion in the 100- and 200-meter **sprint**, as well as in the 4x100 relay, a race in which four runners each sprint 100 meters and then pass the baton to the next runner. He is the first man in the modern Olympic Games to win nine gold medals in the sprint. He is also the first athlete to win gold medals in the 100- and 200-meter races as well as in the 4x100 relay race in three Olympic Games, in 2008, 2012, and 2016. In his autobiography, *Faster than Lightning*, Bolt writes that sports interested him most as a child. He also says that in school he learned something important about himself: he is ambitious because he loves to compete and to win.

He doesn't want to be one of the **runners-up**. This desire to be the best, plus his natural physical speed, brought him to the attention of Pablo McNeil, the former Olympic sprinter who was teaching athletics at Bolt's high school. Pablo McNeil convinced him to concentrate on sprinting and trained him in that sport.

When he was 15, Bolt **launched himself into** world-class athletics in the 2002 World Junior Championships in Jamaica's capital, Kingston. He was so nervous that he put his shoes on the wrong feet! But that was another important lesson: he would never allow stress to affect him again before a race. In spite of his nervousness, he became the youngest World Junior athlete to win the **prestigious** gold medal when he ran in the 200-meter sprint.

At the 2008 Olympic Games, Bolt learned another lesson: he should never stop learning. He broke two records at those games, becoming the fastest sprinter in the 100- and 200-meter race. At the end of the 100-meter race, he shocked everyone when he slowed down before the finish line. He was **ecstatic** because he already knew he was the winner. Some people felt he was too carefree. They thought he should have sprinted all the way. In the following 200-meter race, he didn't slow down. He ran all the way in **record time**, like the fastest man in the world.

B Read the article. Look at the words and phrases in bold in the article. Write definitions or synonyms for each word or phrase.

1. sprint _____
2. runners-up _____
3. launched himself into _____
4. prestigious _____
5. ecstatic _____
6. record time _____

C What factors mentioned in the article do you think have helped Usain Bolt to become a successful athlete?

_____

5 **Write sentences about your regrets. Use *should (not) have*.**

1. I spent all my money on clothes. Now I can't afford to take a vacation.

   <u>I shouldn't have spent all my money on clothes.</u>

2. I was very argumentative with my boss, so she fired me.

   _____

3. I changed jobs. Now I work in a bank. My job isn't very interesting.

   _____

4. I bought a new TV with my credit card. Now I can't afford the payments.

   _____

5. I studied music in school, but I'm much better at computer science.

   _____

6. I was completely rebellious when I was a student, so I got very bad grades.

   _____

7. My friend asked to copy my homework, so I let him. The teacher found out and gave us both Fs.

   _____

8. My cousin invited me to a party. I accepted but didn't put the
   date in my calendar. I forgot all about it.

   _____

9. I was very naive when I was younger. I lent money to people,
   but they hardly ever paid me back.

   _____

10. My friend asked for my opinion on her new hairstyle. I told her I didn't like it.
    Now she's not talking to me.

    _____

6 If . . .

A Rewrite the sentences as hypothetical situations. Use the words given.

1. I should have studied English sooner. (get a better job)

If I'd studied English sooner, I would have gotten a better job.

2. We should have made a reservation. (eat already)

_____

3. I should have put on sunscreen. (not get a sunburn)

_____

4. You should have let me drive. (arrive by now)

_____

5. I should have ignored your text in class. (not get in trouble)

_____

B Write sentences describing hypothetical situations. Use the words given and your own ideas.

Can I borrow the car?

No, you haven't cleaned your room yet.

1. dependable _If I had been more dependable as a teenager,_

my parents would have let me borrow the car more often.

2. ambitious _____

_____

3. pragmatic _____

_____

4. naive _____

_____

5. rebellious _____

_____

6. wise _____

_____

7 **Complete the conversation. Circle the correct time expressions and use the correct tense of the verbs given.**

Hector: I've made such a mess of my life!

Scott: What do you mean?

Hector: If I _____hadn't accepted_____ (not accept)

a job ((as soon as)/ before / until) I graduated,

I _____ around (travel)

South America all summer – just like you did.

You were so carefree.

Scott: You know, I should _____ (not go)

to South America.

I should _____ (take)

the great job I was offered. (After / Before / Until) I returned from South America,

it was too late.

Hector: But my job is so depressing! (Before / The moment / Until) I started it,

I hated it – on the very first day! That was five years ago, and nothing's changed.

I should _____ for another job right away. (look)

Scott: Well, start looking now. I posted my résumé online last month, and five companies contacted

me right away. If I _____ my résumé, no one _____ me. (not post)   (contact)

I accepted one of the job offers.

Hector: Really? What's the job?

Scott: It's working as a landscape gardener. (Before / The moment / Until)

I saw it, I knew it was right for me.

Hector: But for me right now, the problem is that I get a very good salary and I just bought a house.

If I _____ the house, I _____ take a lower paying job. (not buy)   (be able to)

Scott: Well, I guess you can't have everything. If I _____ a better salary, (have)

I _____ a house, too. (buy)

12 Keys to success

1 Complete these sentences with *In order for* or *In order to*.

1. _In order for_ a restaurant to be popular, it has to have attractive decor.

2. _____ a movie to be entertaining, it has to have good actors and an interesting story.

3. _____ succeed in business, you often have to work long hours.

4. _____ attract new members, a sports club needs to offer inexpensive memberships.

5. _____ speak a foreign language well, it's a good idea to use the language as often as possible.

6. _____ a clothing store to succeed, it has to be able to find the latest fashions.

2 Write sentences. Use the information in the box.

☐ have talented salespeople	☐ work extremely long hours
☑ keep up with your studies	☐ provide excellent customer service
☐ be clever and entertaining	☐ have drama and interesting characters

1. be a successful student

   In order to be a successful student, you have to keep up with your studies.

2. a clothes store to be profitable

   For a clothes store to be profitable, _____

3. manage your own business

   _____

4. an advertisement to be persuasive

   _____

5. run a successful automobile company

   _____

6. a reality TV show to be successful

   _____

3 Choose the correct word or phrase.

1. I didn't enjoy this book on how to succeed in business. It wasn't very
   _____well written_____. (affordable / well paid / well written)

2. I learned a lot about how to run a successful bookstore from taking that class.
   I found it very _____. (attractive / informative / knowledgeable)

3. Annie has so many interesting ideas, and she's always thinking of new projects.
   She's very _____. (clever / entertaining / tough)

4. Debra is a salesperson, and she's good at her job. She's so _____
   that she sells three times as much as her co-workers. (unfriendly / affordable / persuasive)

5. Matthew is one of the top models in Milan. He goes to the gym every day,
   so he looks really _____. (clever / charming / muscular)

6. Before opening a new store, it's important to think through all of your ideas and have
   _____. (competitive salaries / a clear business plan / a reliable job)

7. My new job has great benefits. We have unlimited time off, excellent health insurance, and
   _____. (a good product / flexible working hours / a crowdfunding platform)

4 Read this information about journalists. Then write a paragraph about one of the people in the box or another person of your choice.

To be a successful journalist, you need to be both talented and dynamic. You have to write well and write quickly. In order to report the news, a journalist needs to have a good knowledge of world and current events. In addition, you must be able to report a story accurately.

| an artist | a boss | a homemaker | a parent | a teacher |

_____

_____

_____

_____

_____

_____

_____

5 I like it because . . .

A For each pair of pictures, write one sentence about what you like and one sentence about what you dislike. Give reasons using the words given.

1. <u>I like this park because it's clean</u> <u>I don't like this park since</u>

<u>and there are a lot of trees.</u> (because) _____ (since)

2. _____ _____

_____ (since) _____ (the reason)

3. _____ _____

_____ (because of) _____ (due to)

B Think of an example in your city of each of these places: a restaurant, a hotel, and a shopping center. Write a sentence about why you like or dislike each one.

Example: <u>The reason I don't like Cho Dang Gol Restaurant in my hometown is its noisy location</u>

<u>right by the freeway.</u>

1. _____

2. _____

3. _____

6 A new business with an ancient product

A Scan the article about Andean Grain. What is the secret that the company is selling?

SELLING SECRETS OF THE PAST

The Argentinian company Andean Grain is contributing to a **comeback** of highly nutritious foods that were unknown to many people during the last few hundred years. Andean Grain sells foods made from **indigenous** Latin American plants, like chia seeds, amaranth, and quinoa. These plants are coming **to prominence** today because knowledgeable people have discovered that chia seeds, amaranth, and quinoa are **superfoods**, incredibly rich in vitamins and proteins.

Chia seeds were grown by the Aztecs as an energy food. In order to travel long distances without having to stop, they drank a beverage consisting of chia seeds, lemon juice, and water. The Aztecs also cultivated amaranth, which they believed was a superfood, as do scientists today. Quinoa was grown in the mountains of the Andes by the Incas. All three of these foods **went out of favor** after the conquest of Latin America in the 16th century. Wheat was preferred over these native plants, and they were almost unknown outside the countries that grew them. Nevertheless, these foods have become popular once more due to the health benefits that they are supposed to provide.

They appear to be of optimal benefit for the heart and brain, and **rumor has it** that they may help prevent cancer. They're also gluten-free. Because many people today have problems digesting the gluten in wheat, gluten-free foods have become very fashionable.

As a result, there is a great demand by the public for these superfoods. Andean Grain sells its products all over the world, but it is especially active in Europe, where it has a main office in the United Kingdom. From its base in Argentina, Andean Grain sends most of its native plants to Europe to be made into affordable breads, breakfast cereals, and today's popular trail mixes, which are combinations of dried fruits, nuts, and seeds.

The secret is out, and what was hidden from the world for so many centuries has today become an important discovery of foods for our health. Did you know about these superfoods before the rest of the world discovered them just a few years ago?

B Read the article. Look at the words and phrases in bold in the article. Write definitions or synonyms for each word or phrase.

1. comeback _____

2. indigenous _____

3. to prominence _____

4. superfood _____

5. went out of favor _____

6. rumor has it _____

Look at these advertisements and write two sentences about each one. Describe the features and give reasons why you like or dislike the advertisements.

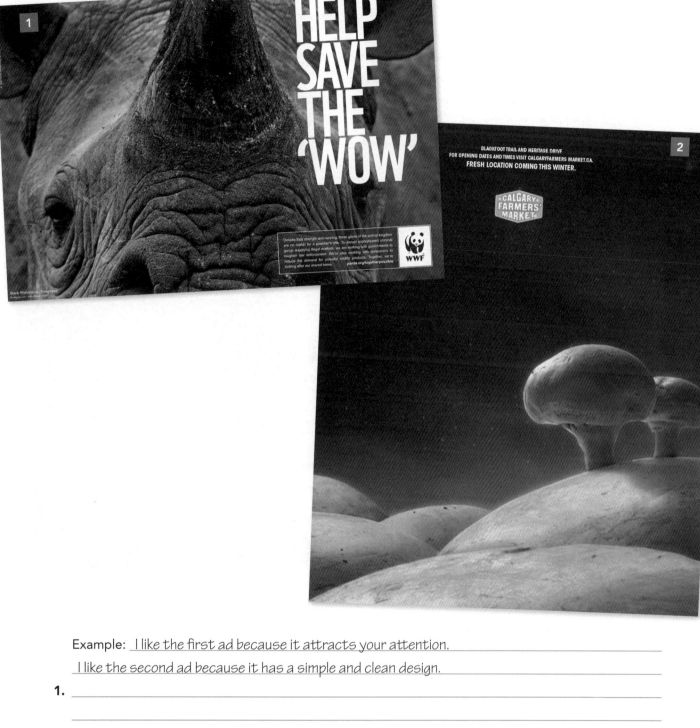

Example: <u>I like the first ad because it attracts your attention.</u>

<u>I like the second ad because it has a simple and clean design.</u>

1. _____
_____
_____
_____

2. _____
_____
_____
_____

8 Do you have the right qualities?

A Complete the sentences with the words from the box.

| affordable | athletic | clever | entertaining | informative | knowledgeable | muscular | salesperson |

1. I'm not _____ enough about tools to be a successful salesperson in a hardware store. I'm familiar with some common tools, but I don't know how to use most tools.

2. To be successful, personal trainers need to be fit and _____.

3. *Weekend Talk* ran for only three months because it was so boring. For a TV show to be successful on Saturday evenings, it really has to be _____.

4. I wouldn't be a good _____ because I'm not very persuasive.

5. I found a fantastic news website this morning. It's really _____. It has very detailed stories about local and international news.

6. For a salesperson to be persuasive, he or she has to be _____ with words.

7. Kate is so _____. She plays soccer, tennis, and basketball, and she's excellent at all three sports.

8. I like this store, but it's not very _____. Even the small items are expensive.

B Write sentences using the words below and infinitive clauses with *to* or *for*.

1. apply for a job / write a good résumé

   _____

2. be an effective personal trainer / listen to your clients' needs

   _____

3. a restaurant / be successful / delicious food at good prices

   _____

4. students / get good grades / study hard and do their best

   _____

5. learn a new language / practice every day

   _____

1 What do you think happened? Write an explanation for each event using past modals.

1. _She may have lost her car key._ _____

_____

2. _____

_____

3. _____

_____

4. _____

_____

5. _____

_____

6. _____

_____

2 Write two paragraphs about something strange that has happened to you. In the first paragraph, describe the situation. In the second paragraph, give two or three explanations for what happened.

> I invited six friends to a barbecue on the beach. I suggested we meet at eight o'clock. They all said they would come and bring some food.
>
> On the day of the barbecue, only two of my friends showed up. I guess my other friends could have overslept, or they might have decided to do something else. Another possibility is that they may have thought I meant 8 P.M. instead of 8 A.M. I'm not sure what happened!

_____
_____
_____
_____
_____
_____
_____
_____

3 Answer these questions. Write two explanations using past modals.

Why do you think the ancient Britons built Stonehenge?

1. They might have _built it to use as a church._

_____

2. _____

_____

3. They could have _____

_____

4. _____

_____

How do you think early explorers communicated with people in the places they visited?

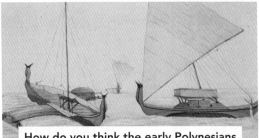

How do you think the early Polynesians were able to travel across vast oceans?

5. They may have _____

_____

6. _____

_____

4 Strange creatures

A Skim the online article about a world-famous legend. Where does the legend come from?

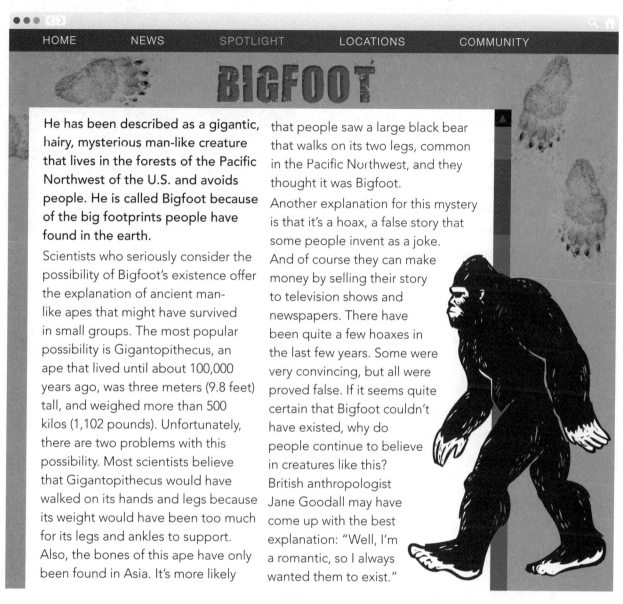

HOME   NEWS   SPOTLIGHT   LOCATIONS   COMMUNITY

BIGFOOT

He has been described as a gigantic, hairy, mysterious man-like creature that lives in the forests of the Pacific Northwest of the U.S. and avoids people. He is called Bigfoot because of the big footprints people have found in the earth.

Scientists who seriously consider the possibility of Bigfoot's existence offer the explanation of ancient man-like apes that might have survived in small groups. The most popular possibility is Gigantopithecus, an ape that lived until about 100,000 years ago, was three meters (9.8 feet) tall, and weighed more than 500 kilos (1,102 pounds). Unfortunately, there are two problems with this possibility. Most scientists believe that Gigantopithecus would have walked on its hands and legs because its weight would have been too much for its legs and ankles to support. Also, the bones of this ape have only been found in Asia. It's more likely that people saw a large black bear that walks on its two legs, common in the Pacific Northwest, and they thought it was Bigfoot.

Another explanation for this mystery is that it's a hoax, a false story that some people invent as a joke. And of course they can make money by selling their story to television shows and newspapers. There have been quite a few hoaxes in the last few years. Some were very convincing, but all were proved false. If it seems quite certain that Bigfoot couldn't have existed, why do people continue to believe in creatures like this? British anthropologist Jane Goodall may have come up with the best explanation: "Well, I'm a romantic, so I always wanted them to exist."

B Read the article. Then write answers to the questions.

1. How might someone describe Bigfoot?

_____

2. Imagine that you have seen a creature resembling Bigfoot. Do you think you would have believed it was Bigfoot? Why or why not?

_____

3. What is the most popular possible explanation for Bigfoot from scientists?

_____

4. What is one problem with this popular explanation?

_____

5. What do you think people might have seen when they thought they saw Bigfoot?

_____

5 Should have, could have, would have

A What should or shouldn't these people have done? Read each situation and check (✓) the best suggestion.

1. Mrs. King wouldn't let her children watch TV for a month because they broke a window playing baseball.

   ☐ She could have made them pay for the window.

   ☐ She shouldn't have done anything. It was an accident.

   ☐ She shouldn't have let them play baseball for a month.

2. Steve's old car broke down on the highway late one night, and his cell phone battery was dead. He left the car on the side of the road and walked home.

   ☐ He should have stopped a stranger's car to ask for a ride.

   ☐ He could have slept in his car till morning.

   ☐ He should have walked to the nearest pay phone and called a tow truck.

3. Sarah was in a park. She saw some people leave all their trash after they had finished their picnic. She did nothing.

   ☐ She did the right thing.

   ☐ She should have asked them to throw away their trash.

   ☐ She could have thrown away the trash herself.

4. Edward's neighbors were renovating their kitchen. They made a lot of noise every day until midnight. Edward called the police.

   ☐ He shouldn't have called the police.

   ☐ He should have realized that they were trying to finish the job quickly.

   ☐ He could have asked them not to make any noise in the evenings.

5. Barbara's boss borrowed $20 from her a month ago, but he forgot to pay her back. Barbara never said anything about it.

   ☐ She should have demanded her money back.

   ☐ She shouldn't have loaned it to him.

   ☐ She could have written him a nice email asking for the money.

B What would you have done in the situations in part A? Write suggestions or comments using past modals.

1. _I would have made them pay for the window._

2. _____

3. _____

4. _____

5. _____

6 Nouns and verbs

A Complete the chart.

Noun	Verb	Noun	Verb
assumption	_assume_	_____	predict
criticism	_____	suggestion	_____
demand	_____	suspect	_____
excuse	_____	warning	_____

B Complete the sentences using words from the chart in part A. For the verbs, use *shouldn't have* + past participle. For the nouns, use the appropriate singular or plural form.

1. Last year some economists said that food and gas prices wouldn't increase. Those _____predictions_____ were wrong! Both food and gas are more expensive now.

2. Christopher _____ having a beach party. It was so dark, I stepped in a hole and hurt my ankle.

3. Andy bought an expensive ring and gave it to Millie for her birthday. A year later, he asked her to marry him. When she said no, he made an outrageous _____. He said he wanted his ring back!

4. I _____ my co-worker not to be late for work so often. It was really none of my business.

5. Lori said she was late because she got caught in traffic. Hmm. I've heard that _____ before.

6. Kevin _____ I would still be awake at midnight. I was asleep when he called.

7. I thought that my roommate had taken my wallet, but I found it at the bottom of my bag. I _____ that my roommate took it. He would never do something like that.

8. James _____ me for wearing jeans and a T-shirt to a friend's party. He always has negative things to say.

7 **Complete these conversations. Use the past modals in the box and the verbs given. (More than one modal is possible.)**

> could have   may have   might have   must have   should have

1. **A:** Where's Luke? He's late.

   B: He ___may have gotten___ (get) stuck in rush-hour traffic.

   A: He's always late! You know, he ___should have taken___ (take) the subway.

2. **A:** Judy never responded to my invitation.

   B: She _____ (not receive) it. You _____ (call) her.

3. **A:** Matt hasn't answered his phone for a week.

   B: He _____ (go) on vacation. He _____ (tell) you, though – sometimes he's very inconsiderate.

4. **A:** I can never get in touch with Kathy. She never returns phone calls or answers texts!

   B: Yeah, I have the same problem with her. Her voice mail _____ (run out) of space. She _____ (get) a new phone service by now.

5. **A:** Thomas is strange. Sometimes he works really hard, but sometimes he seems pretty lazy. Last week, he hardly did any work.

   B: Well, you know, he _____ (not feel) well. Still, he _____ (tell) you that he was sick.

6. **A:** I ordered a book online a month ago, but it still hasn't arrived.

   B: They _____ (have) a problem with the warehouse, but they _____ (let) you know.

14 Creative careers

1 **Complete the conversation. Use the passive form of the verbs given.**

Anna: Putting on a fashion show must be really fun!

Marcus: Yeah, but it's also challenging. All the clothes have to _____be numbered_____ (number) so that the models wear them in the right sequence. And they also have to _____ (mark) with the name of the right model.

Anna: What happens if something _____ (wear) by the wrong model?

Marcus: Well, if it doesn't fit, it looks terrible! First impressions are very important. A lot of clothes _____ (sell) because they look good at the show.

Anna: Do you have to rehearse for a fashion show?

Marcus: Of course! There's more involved than just models and clothes. Special lighting _____ (use), and music _____ (play) during the show.

Anna: It sounds complicated.

Marcus: Oh, it is. And at some fashion shows, a commentary may _____ (give).

Anna: A commentary? What do you mean?

Marcus: Well, someone talks about the clothes as they _____ (show) on the runway by the models.

Anna: It sounds like timing is really important.

Marcus: Exactly. Everything has to _____ (time) perfectly! Otherwise, the show may _____ (ruin).

2 Choose the correct words or phrases.

1. Often, special music has to be _____ for a film.
(written / designed / hired)

2. A play may be _____ for several weeks before it is shown to the public.
(shot / taken / rehearsed)

3. Designing _____ for actors to wear requires a lot of creativity.
(scripts / movies / clothes)

4. Newspapers are _____ to stores after they are printed.
(written / delivered / reported)

5. _____ are added after the film has been put together.
(Scenes / Sound effects / Actors)

3 Complete this passage. Use the passive form of the verbs given.

1. Nowadays, all sorts of things _____*are produced*_____ (produce) in factories, including lettuce!
At one food factory, fresh green lettuce _____ (grow) without sunlight or soil.
Here is how it _____ (do).

2. Lettuce seedlings _____ (place) at one end of a long production line.
Conveyor belts _____ (use) to move the seedlings slowly along. The tiny plants
_____ (expose) to light from fluorescent lamps.

3. They have to _____ (feed) through the roots with plant food and water that
_____ (control) by a computer.

4. Thirty days later, the plants _____ (collect) at the other end of the conveyor belts.

5. They may _____ (deliver) to the vegetable market the same day.

4 Professional fashion blogger

A Scan the article and use the past participle form of the words in the box to complete the sentences with the passive voice.

concern	create	inspire	interest	interview	notice

A Passion for Fashion

In just the last ten years, a new job category has been ¹_____: professional fashion blogger. The story of one of the very first professional bloggers is an inspiration to young people everywhere who are ²_____ with how to make a good living while also doing something that is important to them.

In 2007, Imran Amed, a young Canadian-British citizen who had recently moved to London, decided to take advantage of some free time he had while he wasn't busy working at his job. He sat down in his living room and began to write about something he was passionately ³_____ in: fashion. Sitting on his sofa, he created a blog that allowed him to communicate with readers who shared his fascination with the fashion industry. Naturally, at the beginning, his readers were mainly his friends and family. But because of his ability to tell interesting and perceptive stories that made readers want to keep on reading, his blog was soon ⁴_____ by many people, and by professionals in the industry.

In time, advertisers began to pay Amed's blog, *The Business of Fashion*, for the opportunity to connect with all those readers and potential clients. Amed was also an excellent interviewer. His interviews

with Karl Lagerfeld, Natalie Massenet, Nick Knight, and other giants in the fashion industry became another great attraction to his blog. Designers were willing to be ⁵_____ by him because his questions and comments were relevant, intelligent, and ⁶_____ by his passion for fashion.

Today, professionals in 200 countries consider *The Business of Fashion*

Imran Amed, accepting the Business of Fashion Media Award at the 2016 CFDA Fashion Awards

to be required reading in order to keep up with the latest developments in fashion. Thirty employees now fill the demand for information on fashion. More recent fashion blogs like Chiara Ferragni's *The Blonde Salad* in Italy and Sabina Hernandez's blog *Te lo dije nena (I told you, girl)* in Argentina are now also very successful.

Potential professional bloggers, take note: passionate interest is fundamental to success. If you can discover your passion, then the power of that energy will be the magnet that captures and holds your readers' attention. That is exactly what happened one day when Imran Amed sat down and began to write a blog on his sofa.

B Read the article. Check (✓) the true statements according to the article. For the statements that are false, write the true information.

1. ☐ Imran Amed has always lived in London.

   _____

2. ☐ His family and friends are not interested in fashion and do not read about it.

   _____

3. ☐ Because Imran Amed knows how to tell an interesting story, many people began to read his blog.

   _____

4. ☐ Designers enjoy giving interviews to Imran Amed because his questions are intelligent and show that he is interested in fashion.

   _____

5. ☐ Chiara Ferragni's and Sabina Hernandez's blogs were started before *The Business of Fashion*.

   _____

6. ☐ If you want to be a professional blogger, the most important thing you will need for success is money.

   _____

5 **Join these sentences with *who* or *that*. Add a comma wherever one is needed.**

broadcast presenter

junior newspaper reporter

Examples:

Broadcast presenters are journalists.

They report the news on television.

Broadcast presenters are journalists who report the news on television.

A junior newspaper reporter should be curious.

He or she is often new to journalism.

A junior newspaper reporter, who is often new to journalism, should be curious.

1. An editorial director chooses only the most interesting stories.

He or she tells the reporters what news stories to cover.

_____

_____

2. A game animator is a skilled artist.

He or she creates detailed graphics for computer games.

_____

_____

3. A storyboard artist is a creative person.

He or she illustrates plans for individual scenes for a movie.

_____

_____

4. Stunt people perform dangerous moves in films and TV shows.

The films and shows have a lot of action scenes.

_____

_____

5. TV sitcoms include actors and actresses.

They are recognized by television viewers around the world.

_____

_____

6 Match the definitions with the jobs.

1. a cinematographer __g__
2. a film editor _____
3. a gossip columnist _____
4. a graphic designer _____
5. a club DJ _____
6. a band manager _____
7. a web content manager _____
8. a talk show host _____

a. a journalist who specializes in reporting on the personal lives of famous people

b. someone who plays music in a dance club

c. someone that helps a movie director put together the best "takes"

d. a person who is in charge of choosing the text and pictures on a website

e. a TV personality who invites guests to come on his or her program

f. a person who takes care of business for a band

g. a person who operates the main camera during shooting

h. someone that creates the design for a printed work

7 Choose a job from Exercise 6 or another job you're interested in. In the first paragraph, describe the job. In the second paragraph, explain why the job interests you. Use relative clauses in some of your descriptions.

I'd like to be a band manager for a rock or pop band. Band managers are the people who schedule concerts and shows for bands. They also help bands make creative decisions about things like CD covers, magazine interviews, and even music. In addition, band managers who know people in the music business can help a band become successful.

This job interests me because I love music, and I enjoy being around people who sing and play instruments. Also, I'm organized and reliable, and I think that I have the skills that a good band manager needs.

_____
_____
_____
_____
_____
_____

8 **Describe six steps in the process of renovating a restaurant. Use the passive form of the verbs given below.**

designer

builders

painters

electrician

delivery people

reopening

1. First, _a renovation plan is approved._ (a renovation plan / approve)

2. Next, _____ (new walls / build)

3. Then _____ (the walls / paint)

4. After that, _____ (new lighting / install)

5. Then _____ (new furniture / deliver)

6. Finally, _____ (the restaurant / reopen)

A law must be passed!

1 What should be done about each situation? Write sentences about these pictures, giving your opinion. Use the passive form with *should*, *shouldn't*, or *ought to*.

Leaving large items on the sidewalk

Eating on the subway

Playing loud music in your apartment

Letting dogs run without leashes

1. <u>People shouldn't be allowed to leave large items on the sidewalk.</u>   OR
   <u>People ought to be required to take large items to designated dumps.</u>

2. _____
   _____

3. _____
   _____

4. _____
   _____

2 Make recommendations about the situations in these pictures.
Use the passive form with *has to*, *has got to*, *must*, or *mustn't*.

1. A law has to be passed to prevent people from losing their homes.   OR

Something must be done to repair abandoned homes.

2. _____

_____

3. _____

_____

4. _____

_____

3 Think of four things that you have strong opinions about. Write your opinions and explain your reasons for them. Use passive modals.

Example: _In my opinion, cell phones shouldn't be allowed in class._
They distract students from the lesson.

1. I feel that _____

_____

2. I think that _____

_____

3. In my opinion, _____

_____

4. I don't think that _____

_____

4 Respond to these opinions by giving a different one of your own. Use expressions from the box.

> That's interesting, but I think . . .
> That's not a bad idea. On the other hand, I feel . . .
> You may have a point. However, I think . . .
> Do you? I'm not sure . . .

1. A: Everyone should be required to study Chinese.

   B: _You may have a point. However, I think_
that English is more useful for traveling.

2. A: People mustn't be allowed to write unkind things about others on social networking sites.

   B: _____

_____

3. A: Public transportation should be provided free of charge.

   B: _____

_____

4. A: I think people ought to be required to buy hybrid cars.

   B: _____

_____

5. A: In my opinion, all plastic containers should be banned.

   B: _____

_____

5 Getting revenge

A Skim the web posts. What is a revenge story? Why is each of these stories a revenge story?

DO YOU HAVE A REVENGE STORY? SHARE IT!

1. Marcy: I used to have a friend who was a lot of fun. She always loved to go out to eat. There was just one small problem: Every time the server brought the check, she would say, "Uh-oh! I don't have enough money with me. Can I pay you back later?" This was OK the first and second time it happened, but these excuses happened again and again. I finally got my revenge. The next time we went out for dinner, I said that I had forgotten my wallet. She was shocked, but she paid the check. However, she has never called me to go out again. I guess she was a moocher – a person who always tries to get someone else to pay.

2. Jonathan: My neighbors used to keep rabbits in their yard, but they treated them very badly. Rabbit pens should be cleaned regularly, but these rabbits were dirty, and the smell was really terrible. Worse, I noticed that the rabbits didn't have enough to eat or drink. When I complained to my neighbors, they said, "It's not your problem." When I called the animal protection society, they said they would investigate. I waited a week, but nothing happened. One night, I stole the rabbits and took them home. The next day I gave them to a local pet store.

3. Chad: I was having problems sleeping because of a dripping noise coming from my air conditioner. I thought the air conditioner needed to be repaired, so I called a technician. She couldn't find anything wrong with it, but she said the dripping was coming from the apartment above me. I asked my neighbor to have his air conditioner checked, but he said, "If you can't sleep, that's your problem!" The following day I climbed a ladder and turned off the electricity inside the air conditioner. My neighbor had to call the technician to turn it on, and when she did, she also fixed the dripping. It cost him a few dollars, but it was worth it!

B Read the comments. Do you agree or disagree? Write *A* (agree) or *D* (disagree).

_____ **1.** Marcy shouldn't have pretended to lose her wallet. She should have spoken with her friend and told her it was time she paid for a meal.

_____ **2.** I think Marcy did exactly what she ought to have done. Moochers must be taught a lesson!

_____ **3.** People mustn't be permitted to steal. Jonathan made a big mistake, didn't he?

_____ **4.** If people don't take care of their animals, something has got to be done. However, I don't think he should have stolen the rabbits.

_____ **5.** Sometimes neighbors must be taught a lesson. Chad didn't hurt anybody, so I think his nasty neighbor got what he deserved.

_____ **6.** You may have a point about some neighbors, but I think Chad should have called the manager of his building.

C Do you think getting revenge – doing something mean to someone in return – is acceptable behavior? Why or why not?

_____

_____

_____

6 Add tag questions to these statements.

1. Bullying is a serious problem, _____ isn't it _____?

2. The city doesn't provide enough services for elderly people, _____ does it _____?

3. You can easily spend all your money on food and rent, _____?

4. Some unemployed people don't really want to work, _____?

5. Health care is getting more and more expensive, _____?

6. There are a lot of homeless people downtown, _____?

7. Some schools have overcrowded classrooms, _____?

8. Laws should be passed to reduce street crime, _____?

7 Nouns and verbs

A Complete the chart.

Noun	Verb	Noun	Verb
advertisement	_advertise_	_____	pollute
_____	bully	prohibition	_____
_____	improve	provision	_____
offense	_____	_____	require
permission	_____	_____	vandalize

B Write sentences with tag questions using words from the chart. Use four of the nouns and four of the verbs.

1. _Bicyclists should be required to wear helmets,_ _____

shouldn't they? _____

2. _____

3. _____

4. _____

5. _____

6. _____

7. _____

8. _____

9. _____

8 Give one reason for and one reason against these opinions.

1. Children should be made to study a foreign language in primary school.

    For: _It would help children understand other cultures._

    Against: _I don't think it would be easy to find enough teachers._

2. Schools should punish students who bully other children.

    For: _____

    Against: _____

3. More tax money ought to be spent on cleaning up vandalism.

    For: _____

    Against: _____

4. Stray animals should be cared for in animal shelters.

    For: _____

    Against: _____

9 Complete the conversation. Use passive modals and tag questions.

Gina: You know, I just moved into this new apartment building, and I thought everything would be really great now.

Alec: What's the problem?

Gina: Well, yesterday, the manager gave me a copy of the house rules. I found out that I can't park my moped on the sidewalk in front of the building anymore.

Alec: But people shouldn't _____ (permit) to park their bikes or mopeds there.

Gina: Why not? There isn't any other place to park, _____? I guess I'll have to park on the street now.

Alec: I'm sorry that parking somewhere else will be inconvenient, but don't you agree that people shouldn't _____ (allow) to block the sidewalk or the entrance to the building?

Gina: Well, you may have a point, but parking spaces for all types of cycles need _____ (provide) for renters here. All renters with a car have a parking space, _____?

Alec: Well, yes, you're right. You should go to the next renters' meeting and discuss the issue with everyone else.

Gina: That's not a bad idea. My voice ought _____ (hear) as much as anyone else's – I think I will!

16 Reaching your goals

1 Match each profession with the correct achievement.

☐ actor   ☐ student   ☐ volunteer
☐ parent   ☐ nurse   ☑ high school counselor

1. I've managed to help hundreds of students get into college. <u>high school counselor</u>
2. I was able to clean litter from dozens of beaches over the last three years. _____
3. I managed to maintain an A average during my last four years of school. _____
4. I've been able to work with many of my favorite movie stars. _____
5. I've managed to teach my children how to be responsible citizens. _____
6. I've been able to help sick people feel better. _____

2 Choosing a job

A Complete the chart with your own ideas.

Job	Goals of people with this profession	
1. social worker	help people	_____
2. university professor	educate people	_____
3. small-business owner	_____	_____
4. emergency-room nurse	_____	_____

B Complete these sentences with your ideas from part A. Try to add more details.

1. As a social worker, Jane hopes she'll <u>have helped poor and elderly people in her community.</u>
   She'd also like to have _____

2. As a university professor three years from now, Paul hopes he'll have _____
   _____
   He'd also like to have _____
   _____

3. By this time next year, Jake, a small business owner, would like to have _____
   _____
   In addition, he hopes he'll have _____
   _____

4. In the next five years, Amy, an emergency-room nurse, hopes she'll have _____
   _____
   In addition, she'd like to have _____

3 Write two paragraphs about an issue that is important to you. In the first paragraph, describe a past achievement related to that issue. In the second paragraph, describe a goal.

Last year, I began volunteering at a local animal shelter. I managed to help find homes for over twenty cats and dogs in one year. It was an incredibly rewarding experience.

In the next few years, I hope to help more animals find homes. I'd like to have placed a hundred pets in homes over the next four years.

_____
_____
_____
_____
_____
_____
_____
_____
_____

The challenge of a lifetime

A Scan the first paragraph of the article. Where is Rupert Isaacson from? Where are his parents from? Where did he go?

RUPERT ISAACSON

Rupert Isaacson is a man who has faced a major challenge in his life. The son of parents who were born in Africa, he grew up in London and in the English countryside, where he discovered his love of horses. Because he grew up hearing so many fascinating memories about Africa from his parents, he went there and lived with nomadic people called the Bushmen of the Kalahari Desert. He then wrote a book, *The Healing Land*, about his experiences with the Bushmen and the problems of survival they face in the twenty-first century.

By the year 2000, Rupert was already managing to make a living as a journalist, writing articles and guidebooks about Africa and India. It was in India that he met his wife, Kristin. Today, they live with their son, Rowan, just outside of Austin, Texas, in the U.S. But Rupert faced the greatest challenge of his life when, at the age of two, Rowan was diagnosed with autism, a condition that affects people's ability to communicate and interact socially with others.

Rupert discovered that spending time with horses and riding them was helping Rowan. The presence of the horses was very calming to the boy. Rupert also knew that the Bushmen of the Kalahari possessed great knowledge about healing. He thought that if he could find a group of people with healing powers and a great knowledge of horses, there could be a possibility of helping his son. Unfortunately, the Bushmen of the Kalahari do not have horses.

So the family set off for Mongolia, where horses have been important for thousands of years. Rupert has written about this journey dedicated to helping his son in *Horse Boy*, and he has produced a documentary of the same name. In the film, viewers have the opportunity to see the family traveling in Mongolia, riding horses, and meeting healers in order to help Rowan.

Because working with horses has helped Rowan, Rupert established The Horse Boy Foundation at his ranch in Texas. It is a school that teaches people how to use horses for healing. In addition to writing another book, *The Long Ride Home*, about traveling with Rowan to Africa, Australia, and Arizona in the U.S., Rupert has also produced the documentary *Endangerous*, with Rowan as host, about dangerous animals that are threatened with extinction. Rupert Isaacson has managed to discover the secret of turning one challenge into many accomplishments.

B Read the article. What is the challenge that Rupert Isaacson faced? What was one of the solutions to this challenge that Rupert found?

Challenge: _____

Solution: _____

C Answer the questions.

1. How does autism affect people?

    _____

2. Why did Rupert's family go to Mongolia?

    _____

3. What is the purpose of The Horse Boy Foundation?

    _____

4. What does Rowan do in *Endangerous*?

    _____

5. List three accomplishments of Rupert Isaacson.

    _____

5 Choose the correct word.

1. It's not good to be _____
if you're an emergency-room nurse.
(courageous / timid / upbeat)

2. If teachers are going to be successful, they
have to be _____.
(dependent / rigid / resourceful)

3. You have to be _____
if you work as a volunteer.
(adaptable / cynical / unimaginative)

4. If you take a job far from your family and friends,
you have to be _____.
(compassionate / dependent / self-sufficient)

5. One of the most important things about
working with children is being positive
and not _____.
(adaptable / cynical / resourceful)

6. Being a role model for troubled youths
requires someone who is strong and

_____.

(compassionate / insensitive / timid)

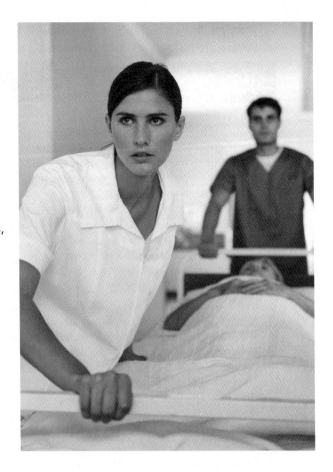

6 Read each sentence. Write *A* for achievement or *G* for goal.

1. I've been able to provide clean water to
three villages during my time as a Peace
Corps volunteer. _____

2. By the time I'm 35, I'd like to have lived
in a culture that's very different from
my own. _____

3. While I was working abroad in
Tokyo, I managed to learn to speak
Japanese fluently. _____

4. After my time with Habitat for Humanity,
I hope to have made a significant and
positive difference in people's lives. _____

5. I'd like to have gotten another degree in
two years. _____

6. I hope I'll have gotten married by the
time I'm 30. _____

7 Accomplishments and goals

A Match the verbs with the nouns. Write the collocations. (More than one answer may be possible.)

Verb	Noun
buy	a change
get	debts
learn	a house
make	a promotion
meet	new skills
pay off	someone special

1. <u>   buy a house   </u>
2. _____
3. _____
4. _____
5. _____
6. _____

B Write one sentence about an accomplishment and another sentence about a goal. Use the words in part A and your own ideas.

1. <u>My sister and her husband have managed to save enough money to buy a house. I expect to have bought a house within five years.</u>

2. _____
_____
_____
_____

3. _____
_____
_____

4. _____
_____
_____
_____

5. _____
_____
_____
_____

6. _____
_____
_____
_____

8 Personal portraits

A Write three sentences about the accomplishments of someone you know very well. Use the present perfect or simple past.

> By investing his money carefully, my neighbor Enrico was able to retire at 40. Since then, he has managed to set up an organization that helps find jobs for people who are homeless. In addition, he has volunteered his time at a homeless shelter in the city.

_____

_____

_____

_____

B Write three sentences about things the same person would like to have achieved in ten years. Use the future perfect or *would like to have* + past participle.

> Enrico would like to have started an organization to provide scholarships for needy college students by the time he's 50. He hopes to travel a lot, too. In fact, he hopes he'll have traveled all through Southeast Asia.

_____

_____

_____

_____